ADULT COLORING SERIES
volume one
FLOWERS AND SOUND

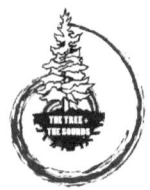

TROY A. STANDEFER

thetreeandthesounds.com

 thetreeandthesounds@gmail.com

www.facebook.com/thetreeandthesounds

www.instagram.com/tree_sounds

@tree_soundz

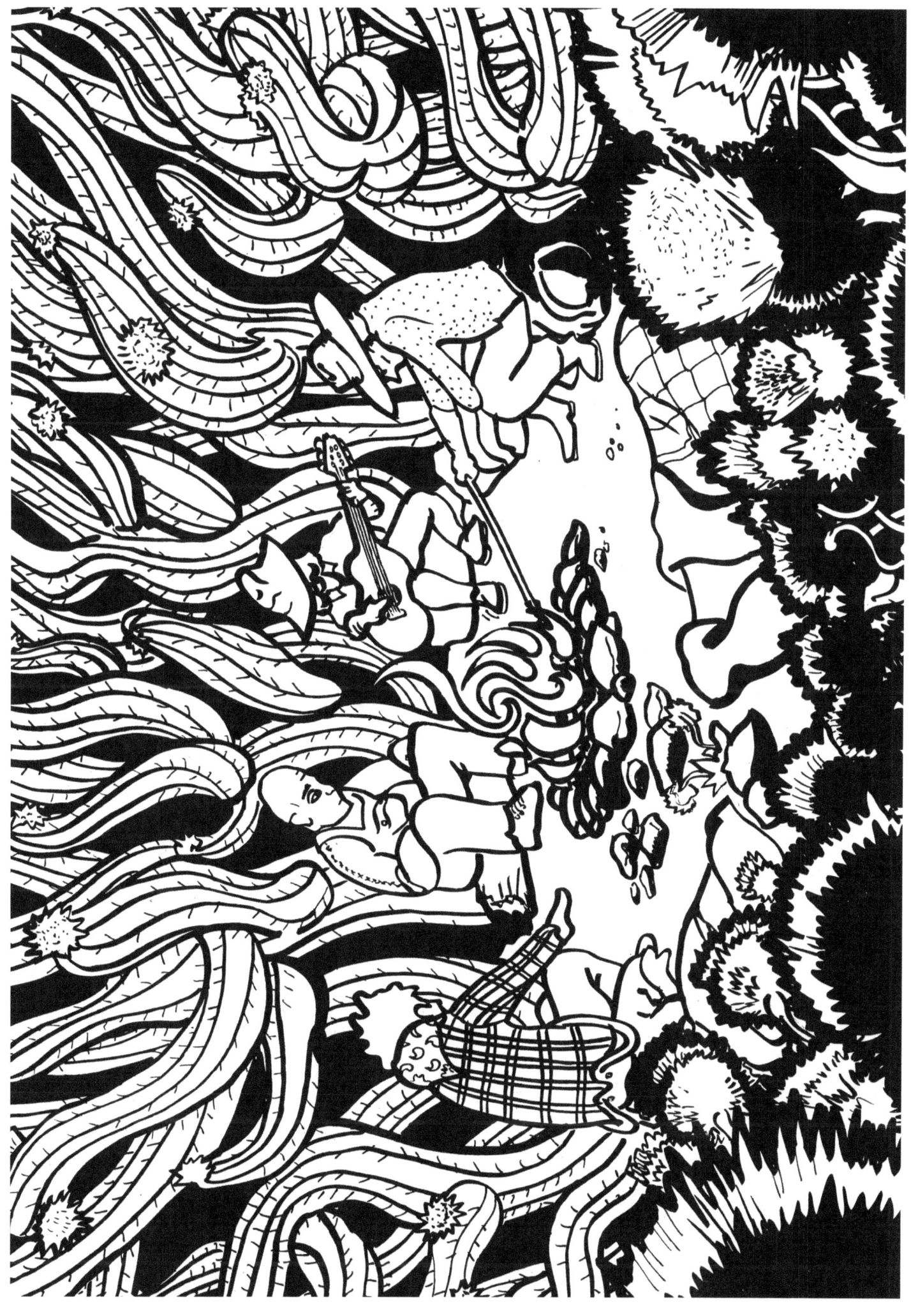

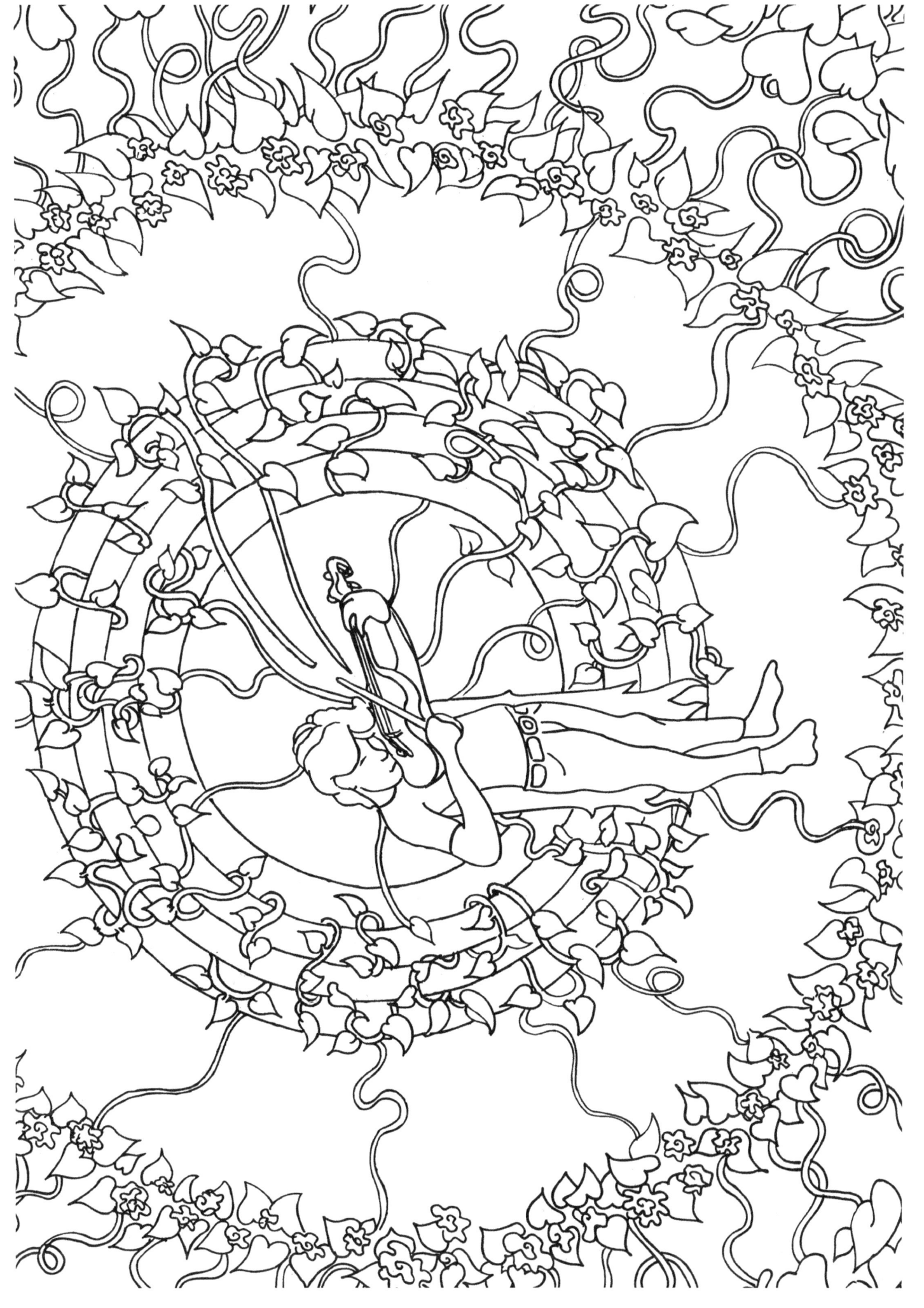

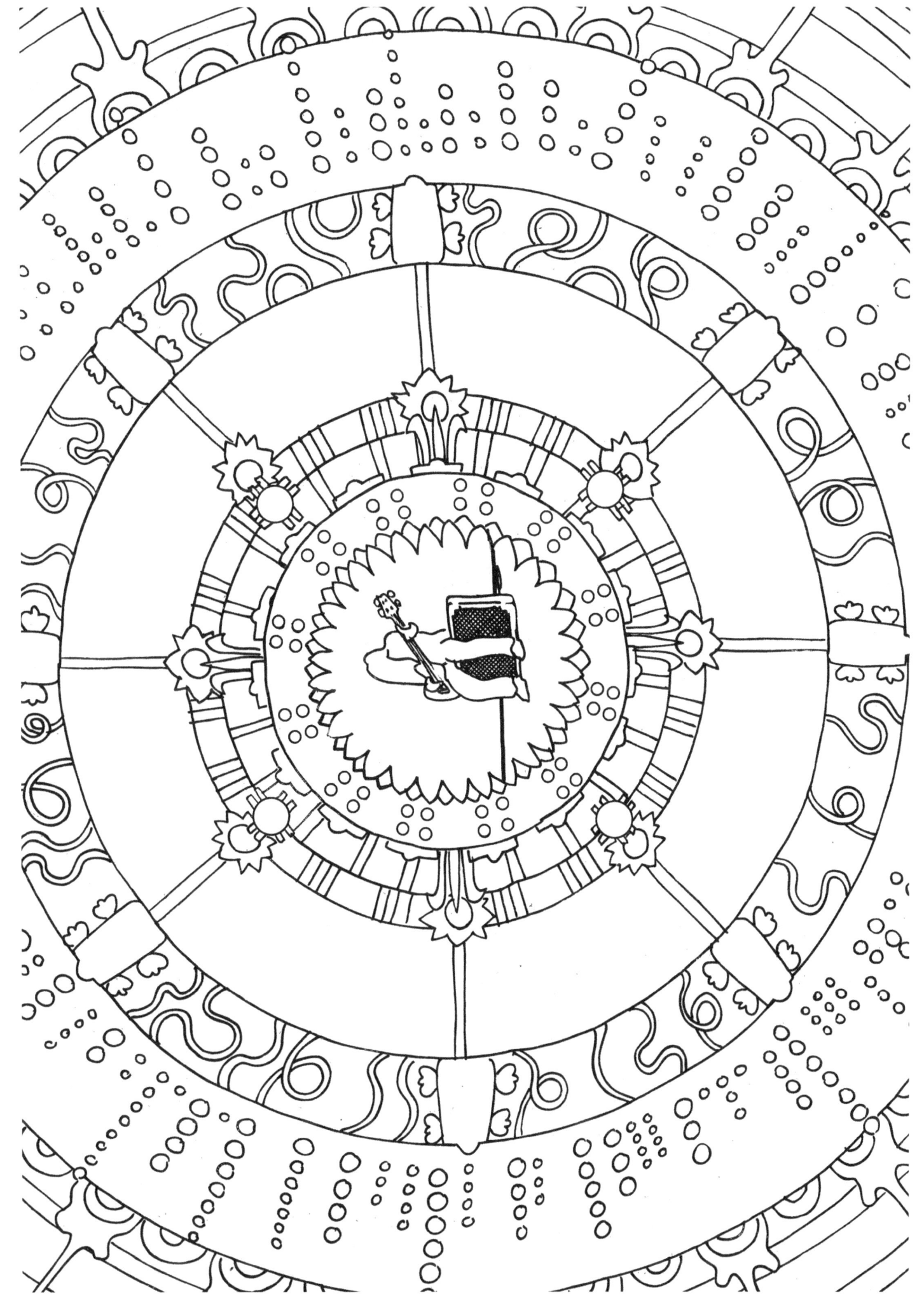

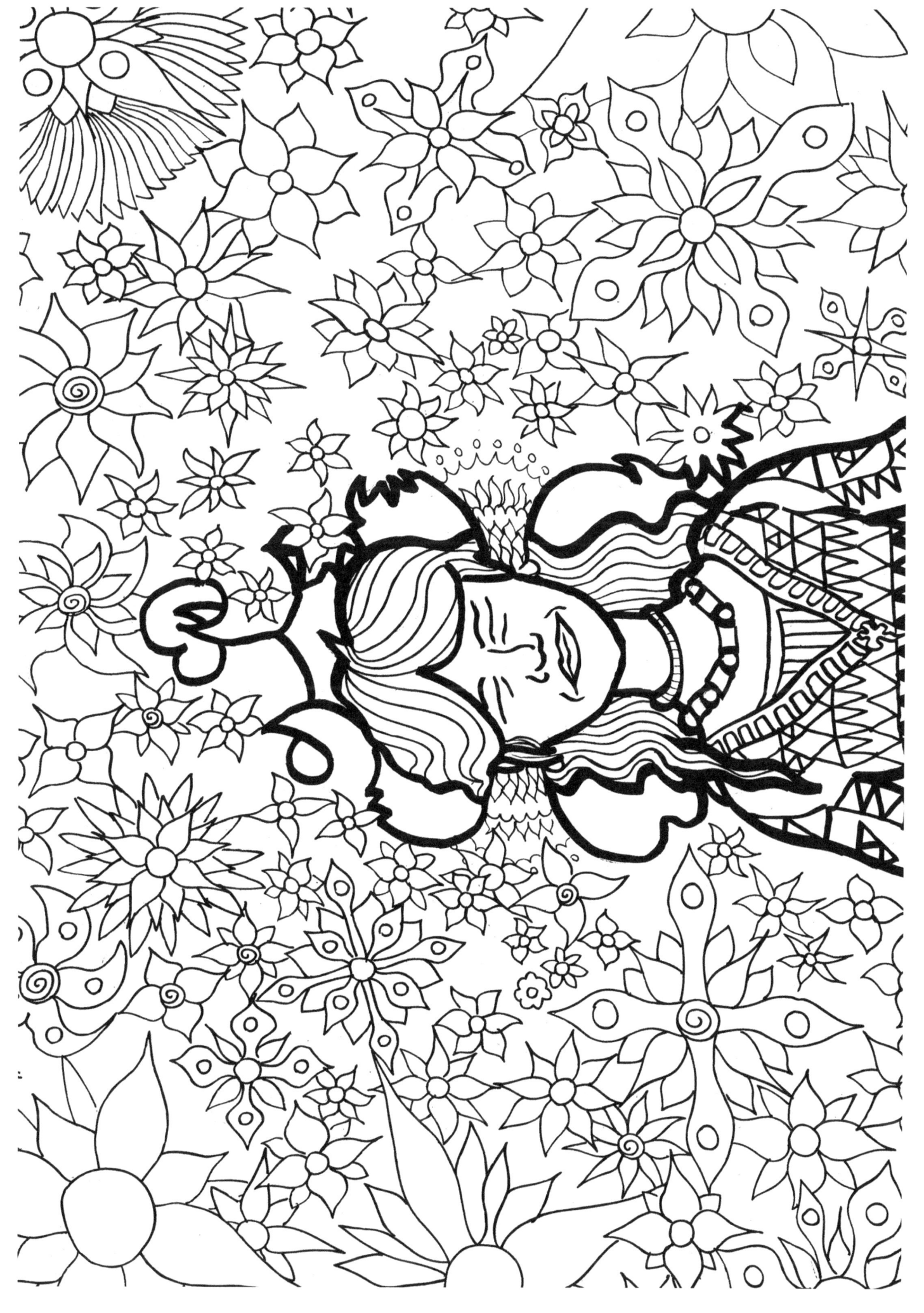

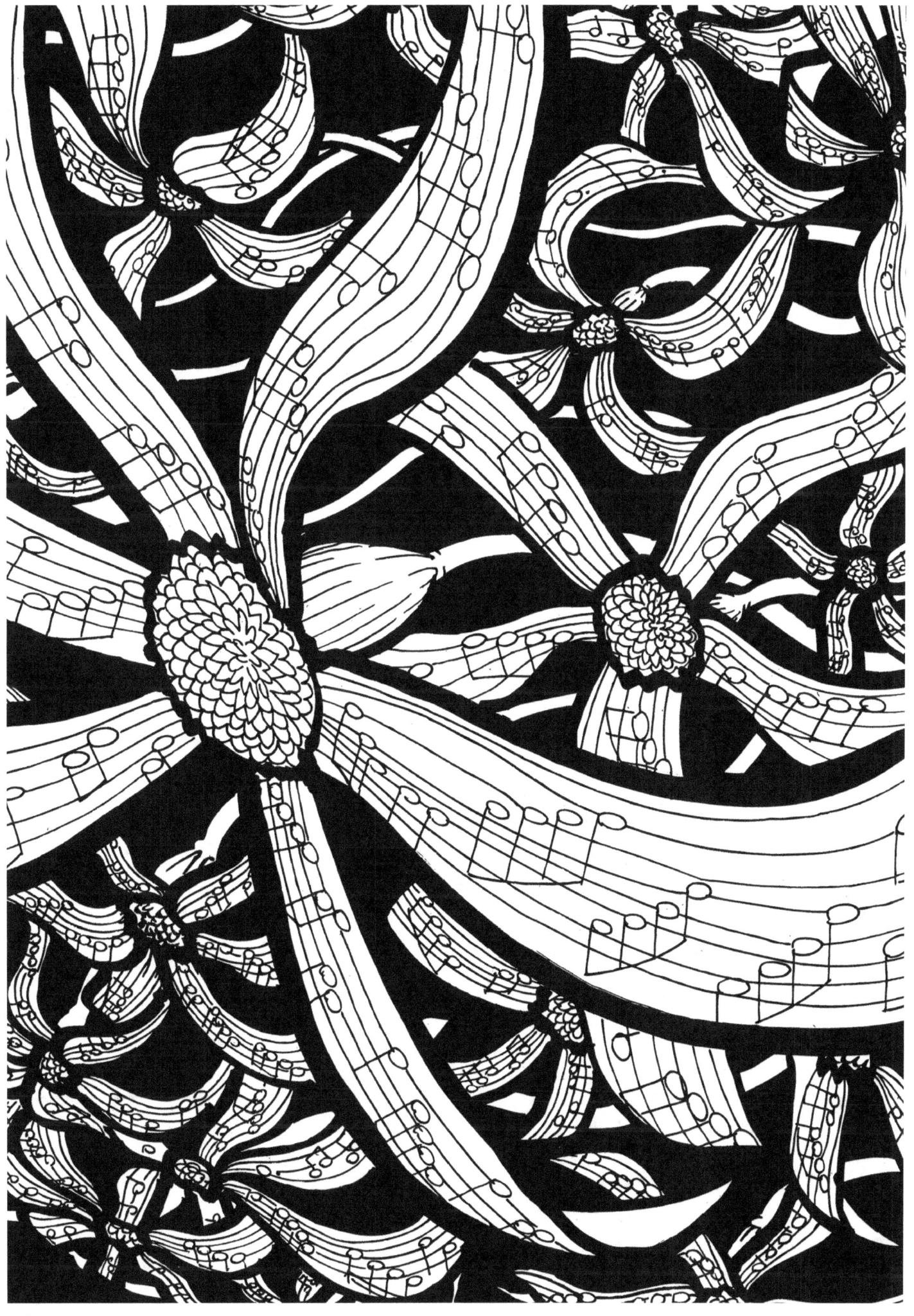

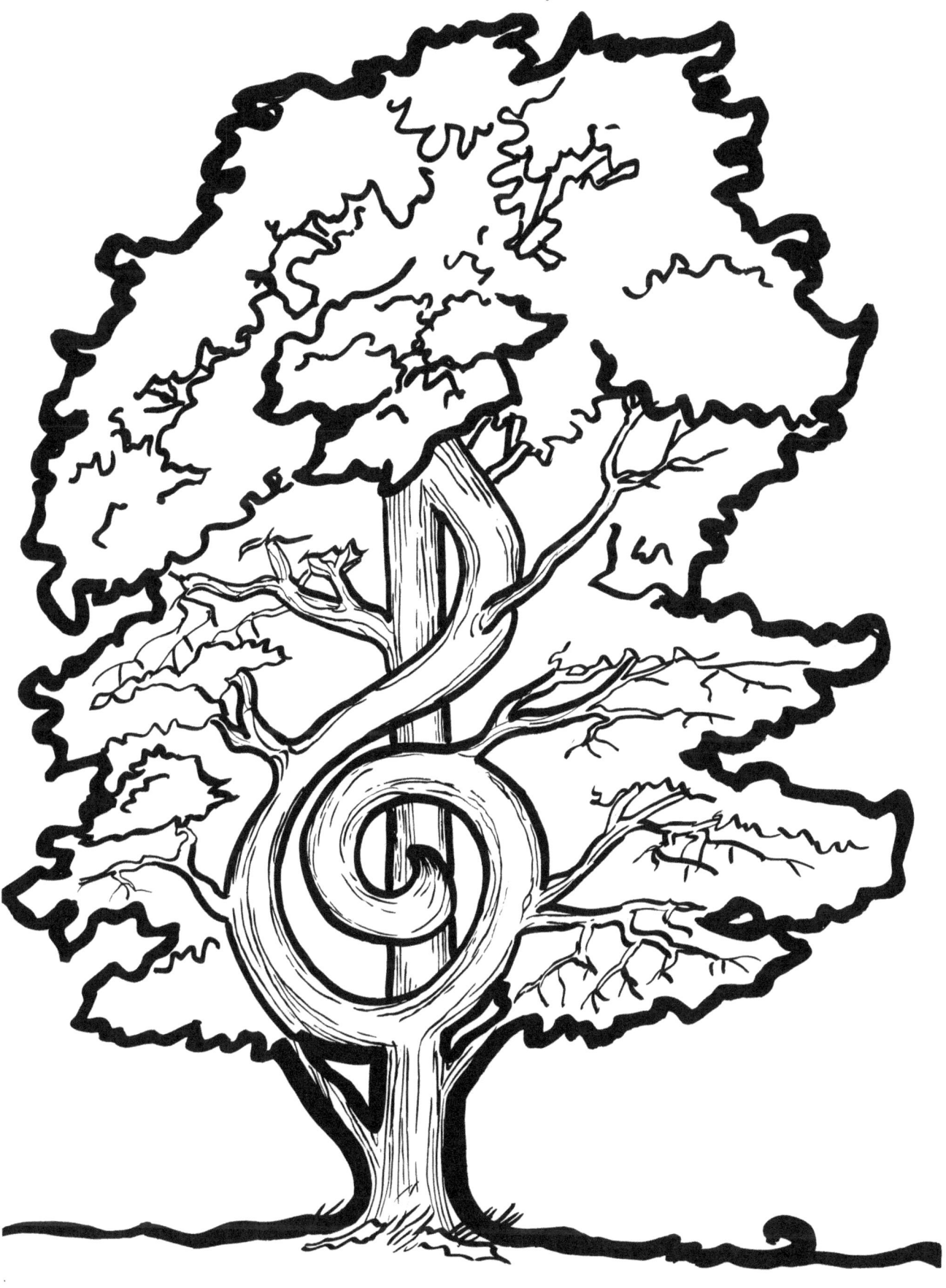

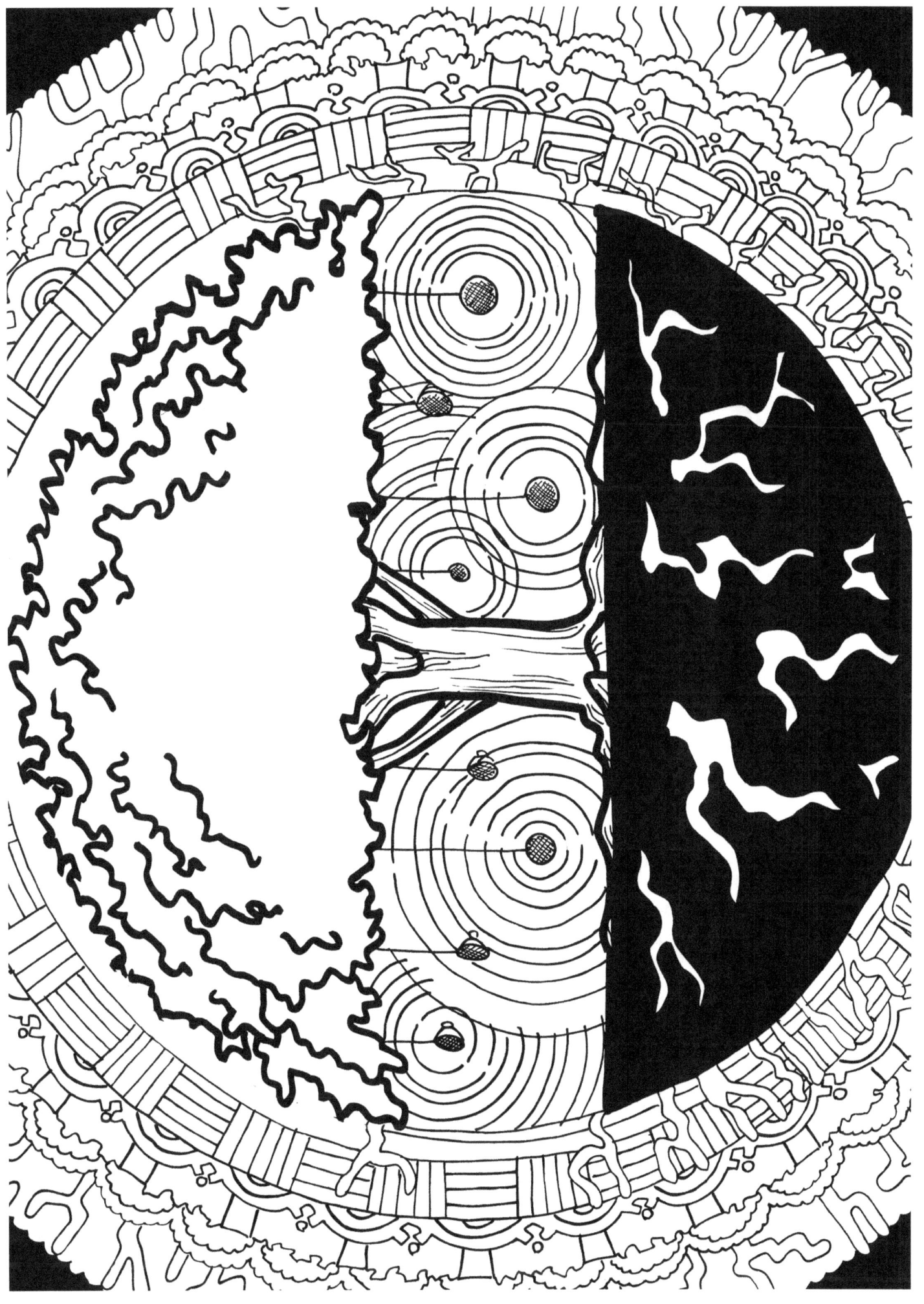

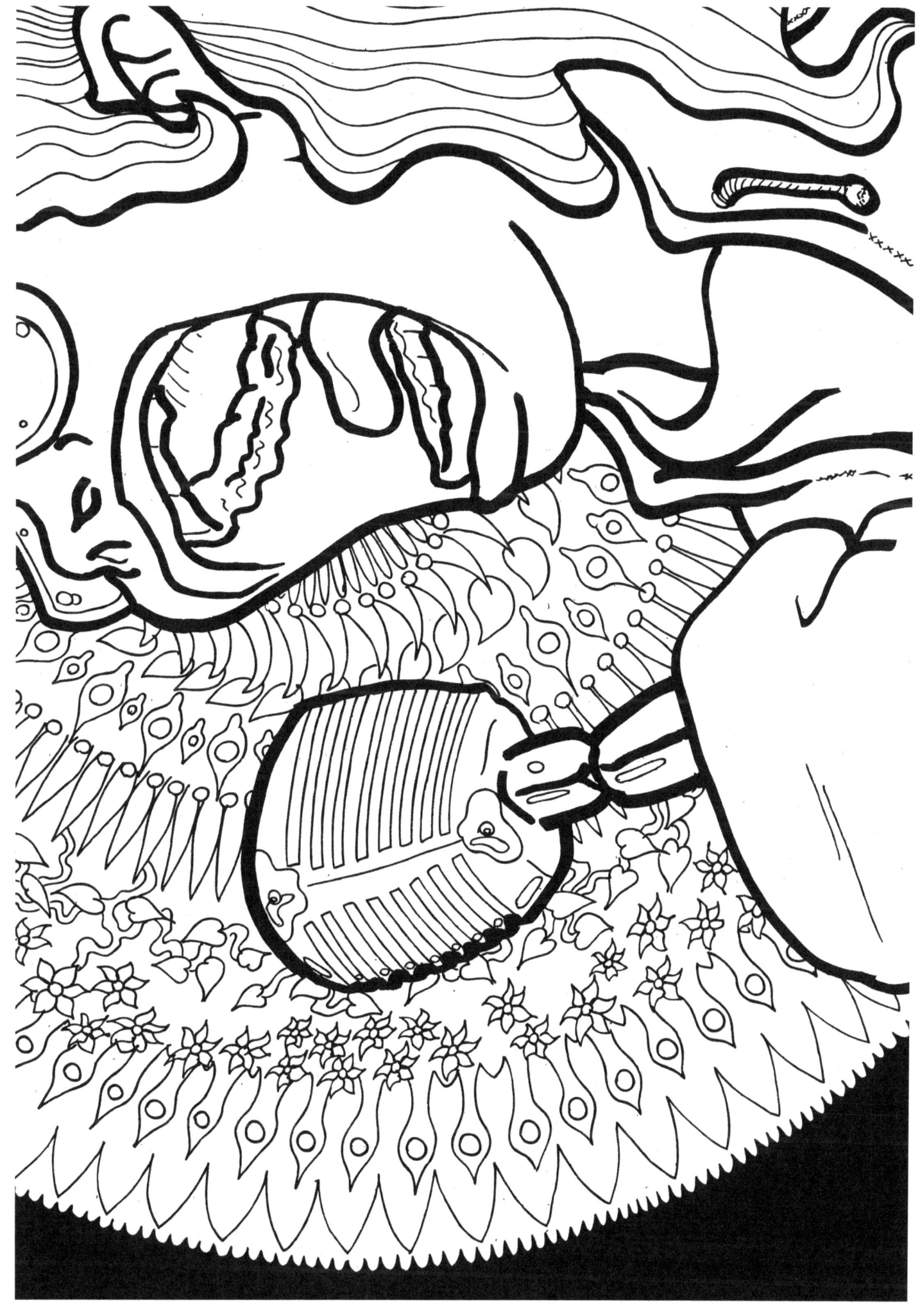

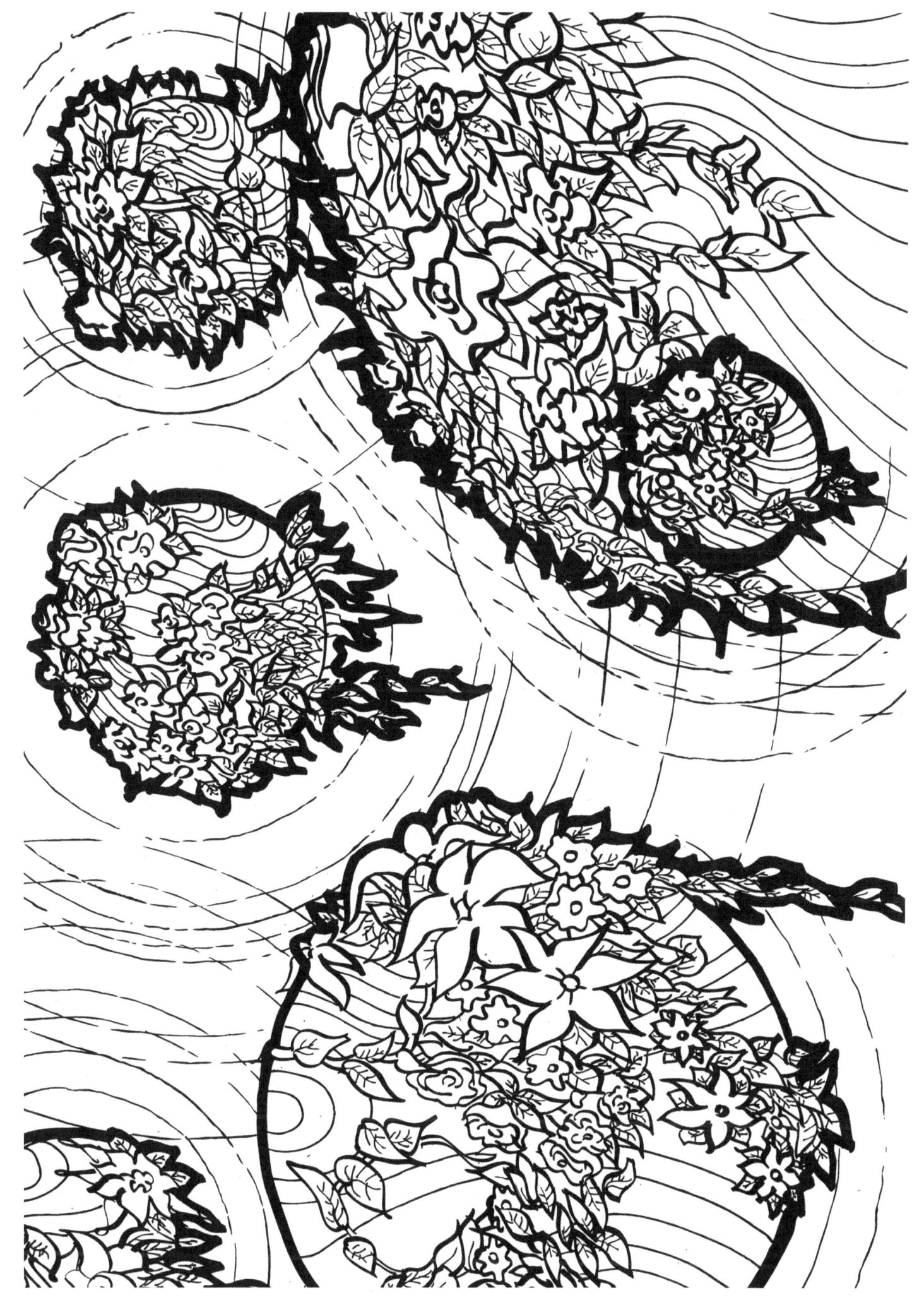

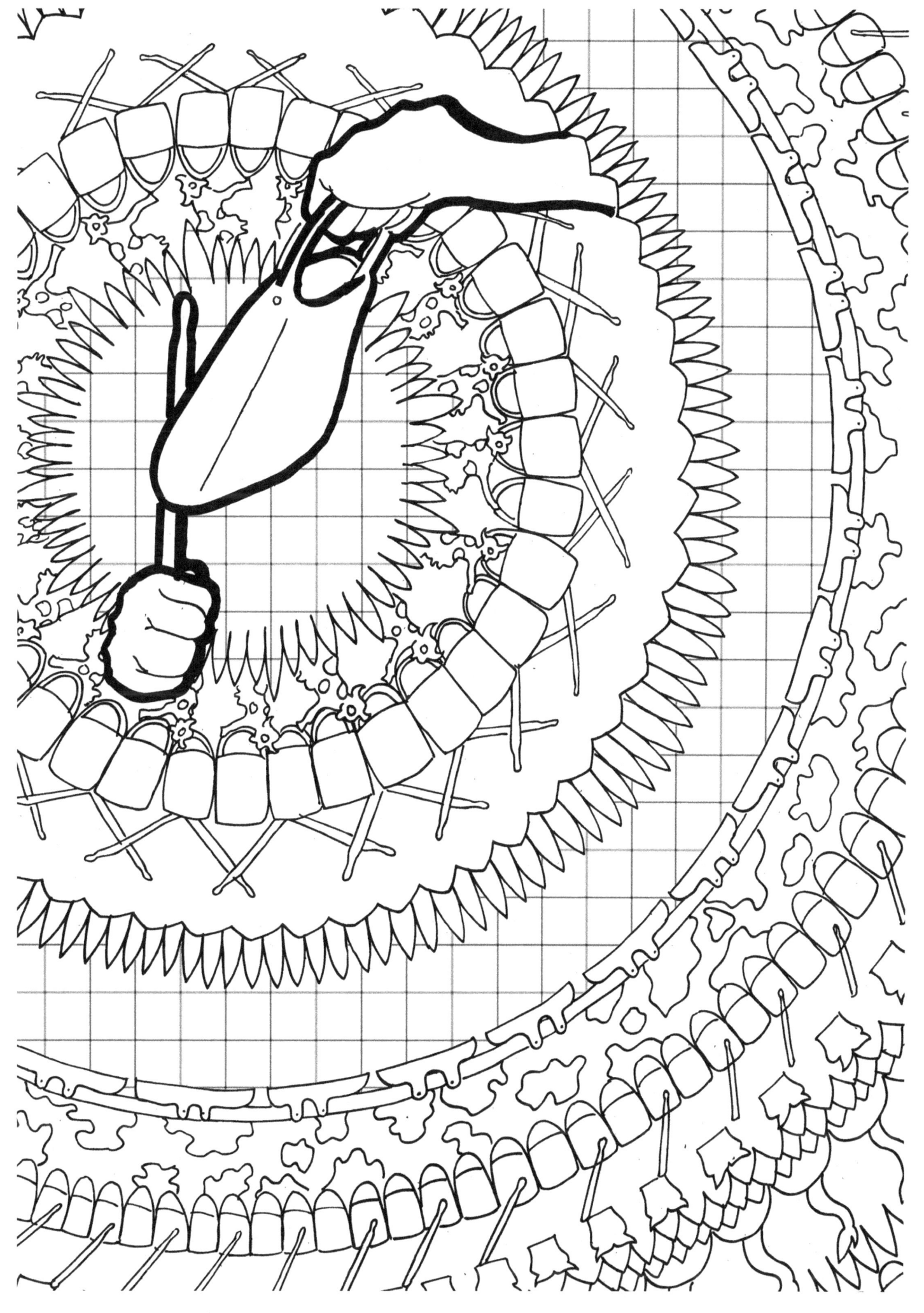

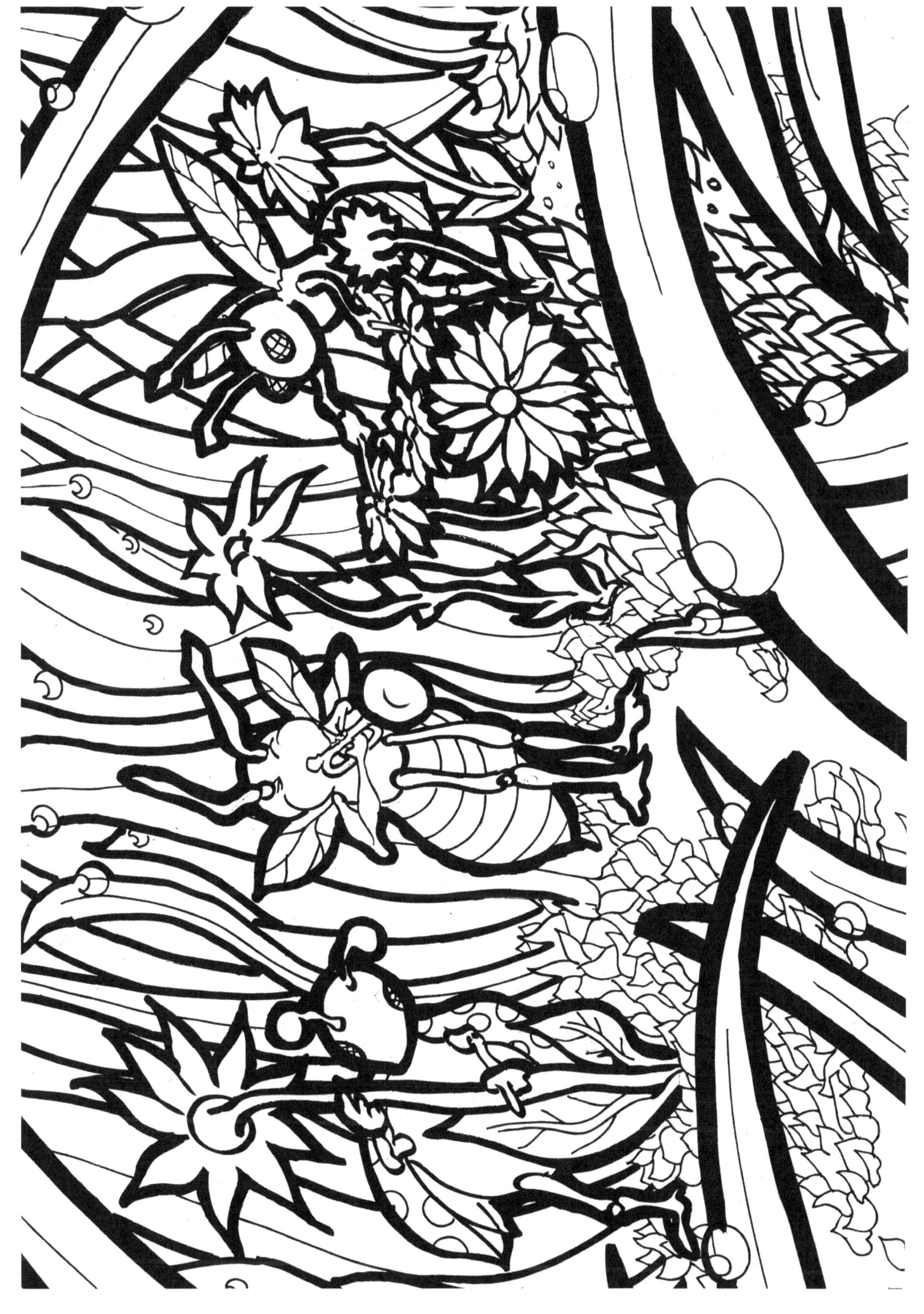

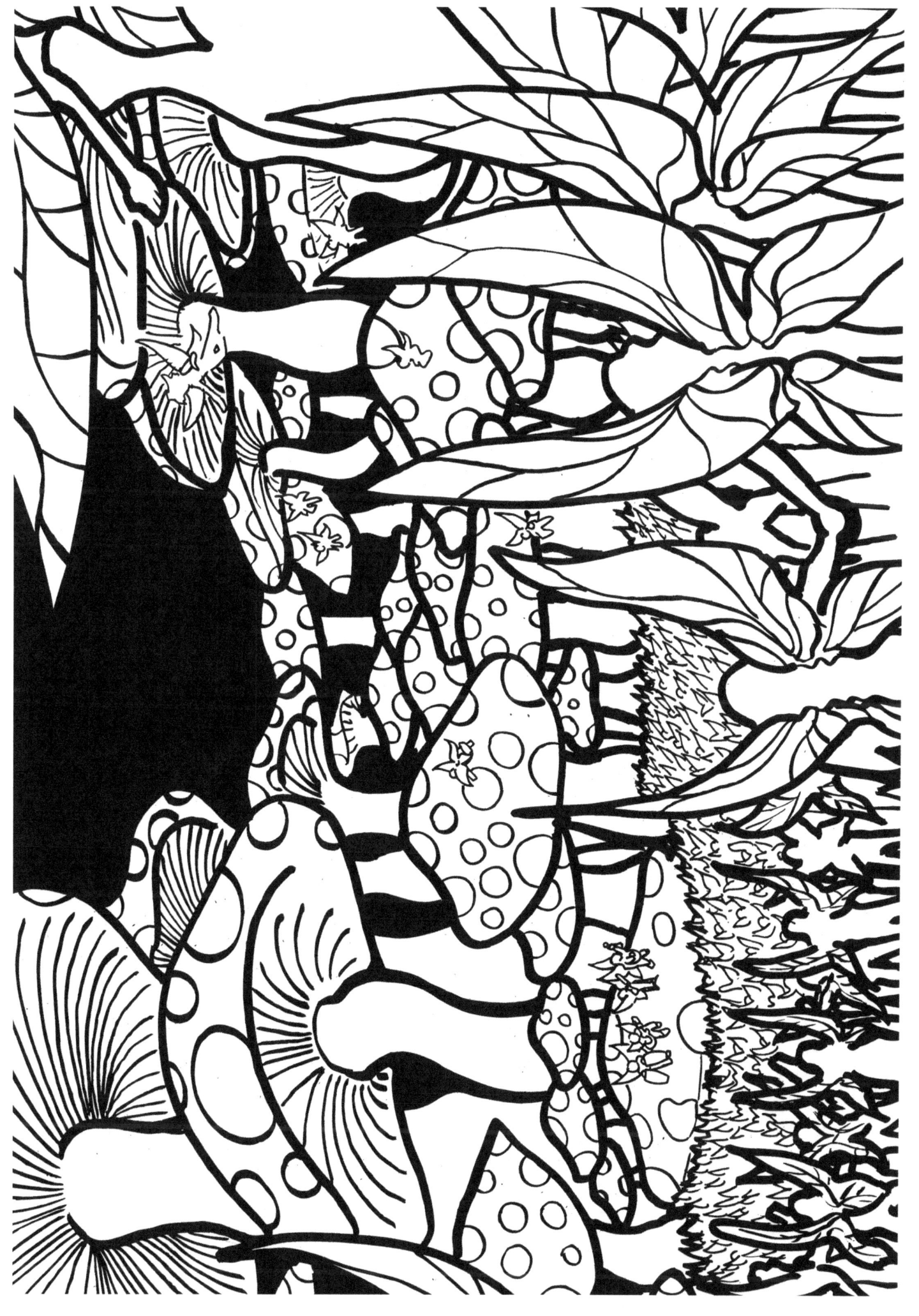

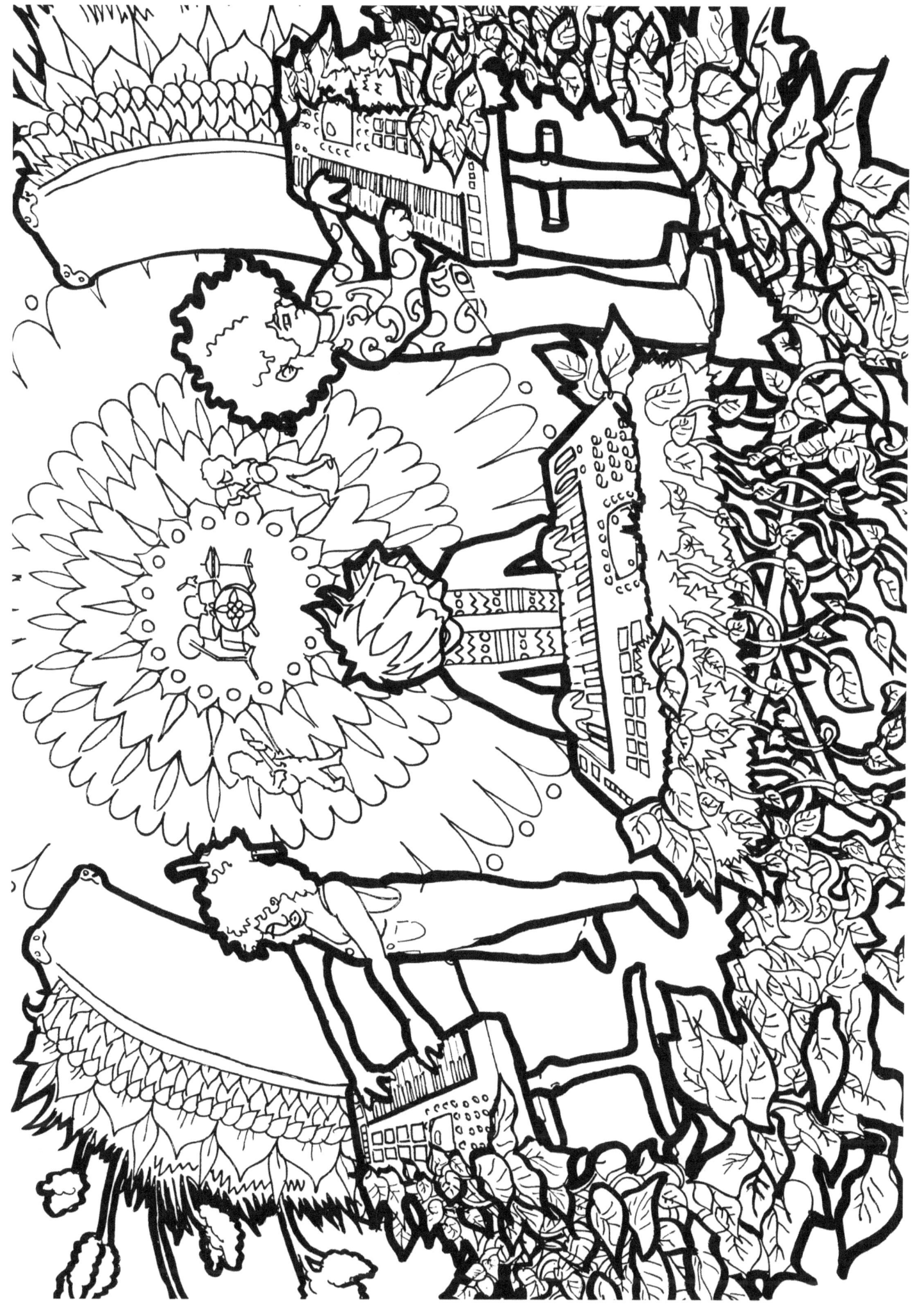

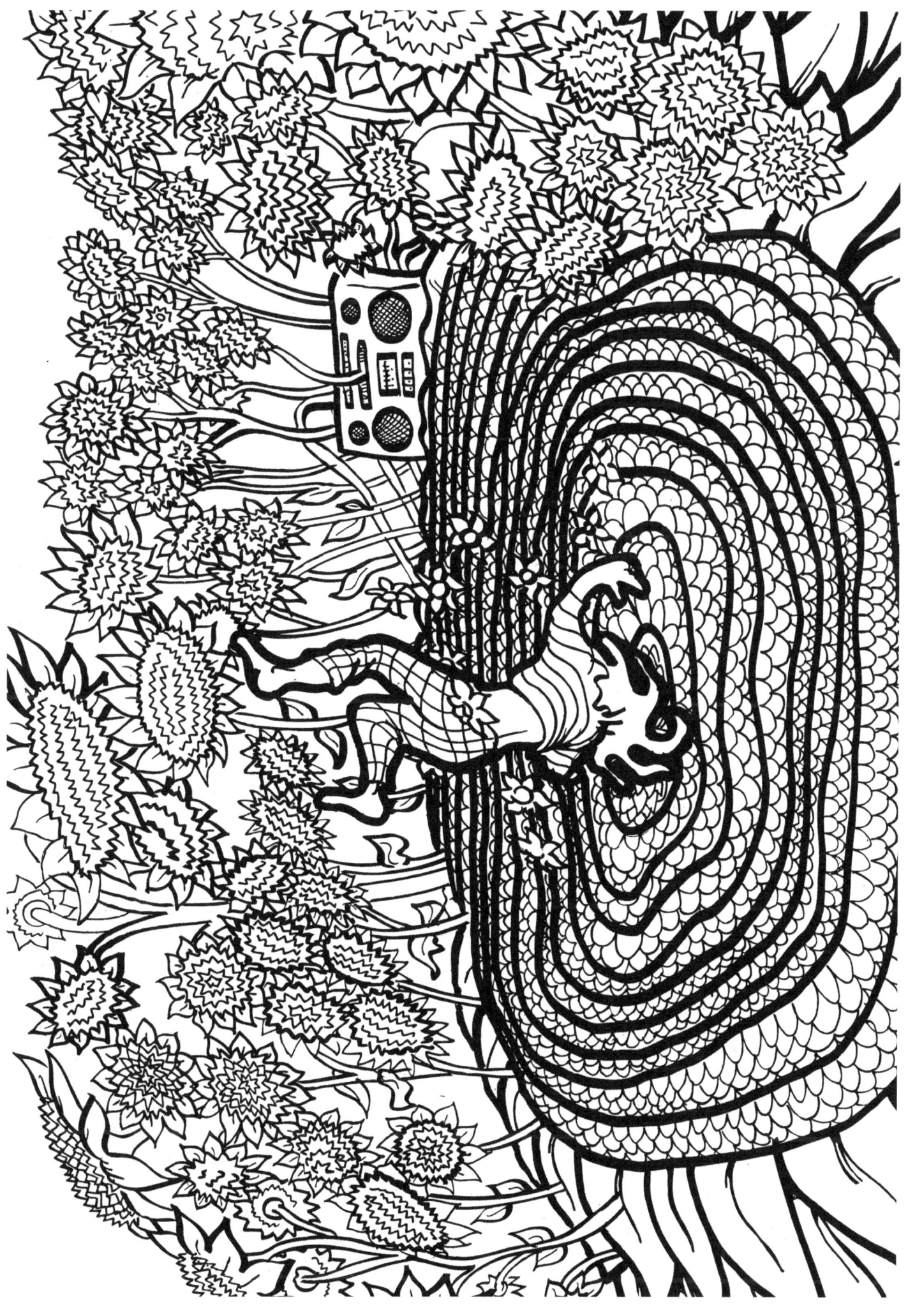

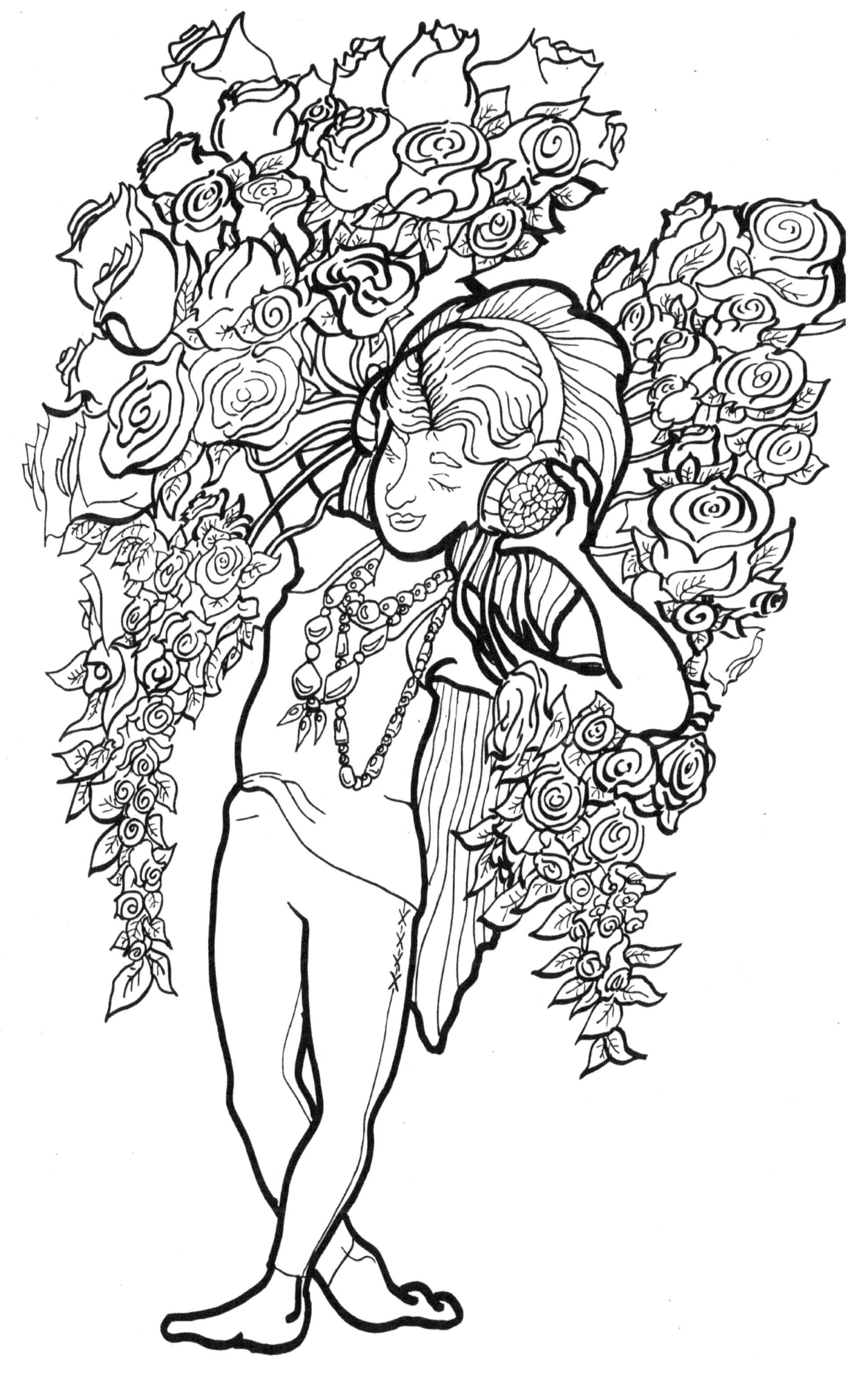

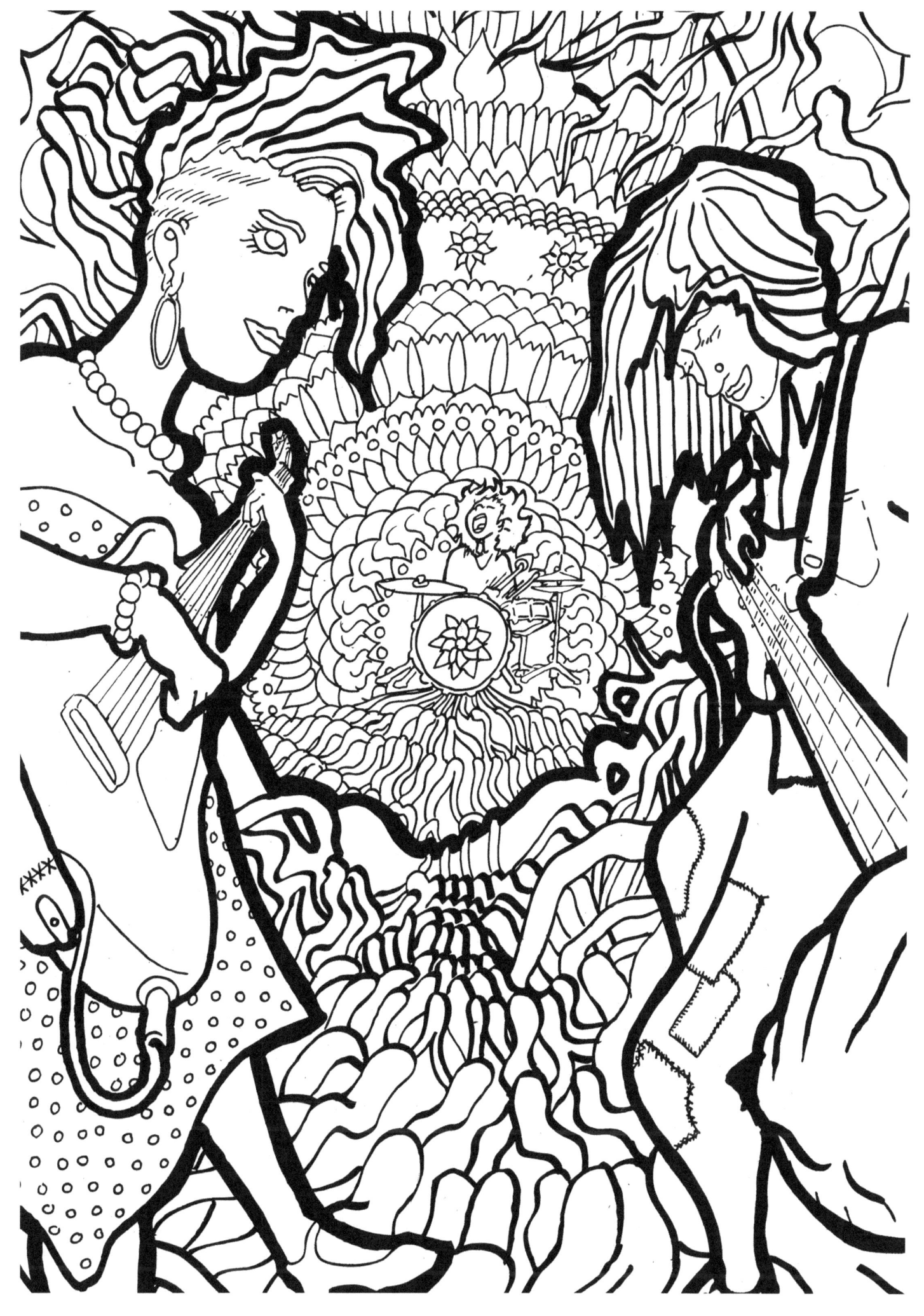

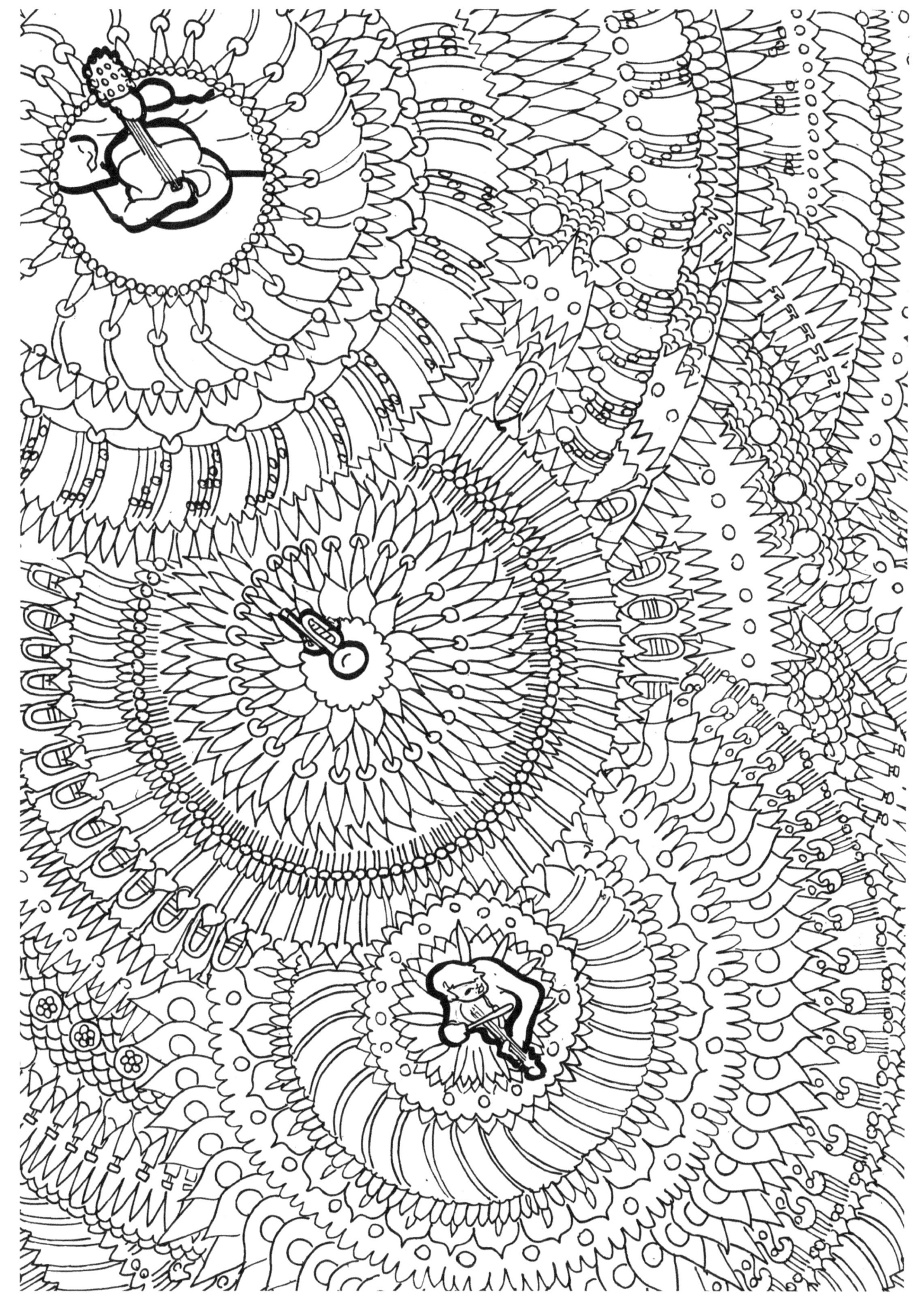

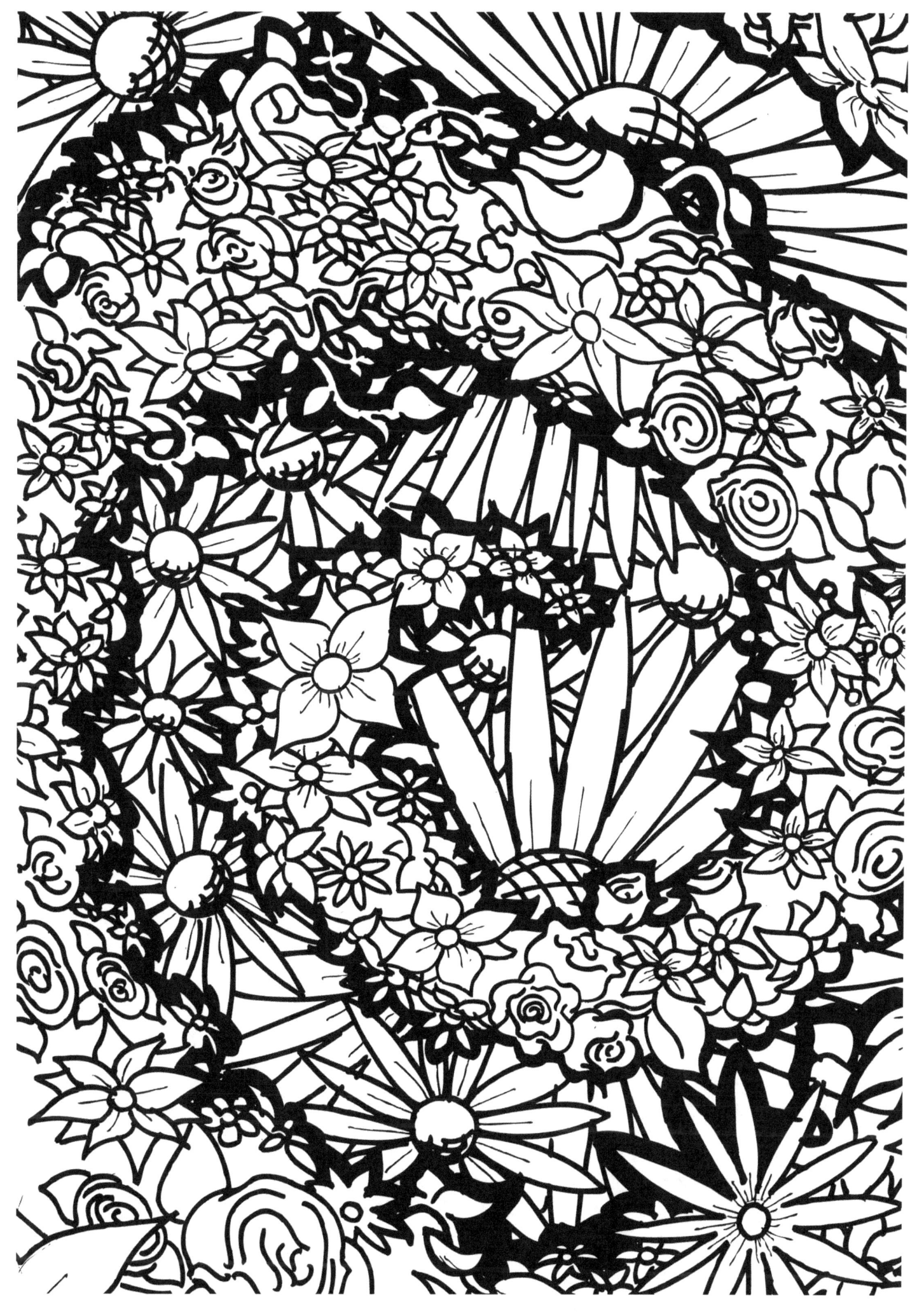

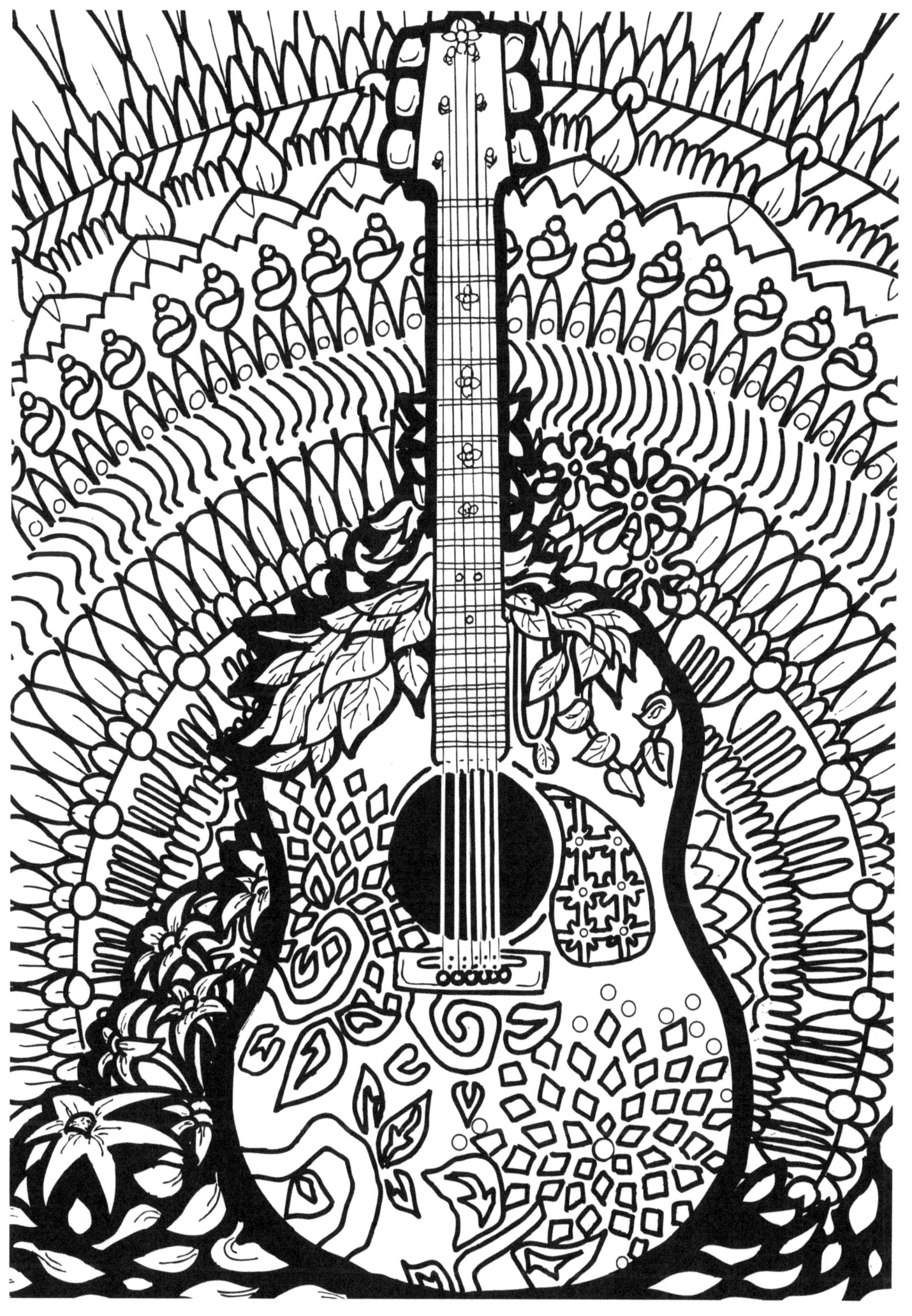

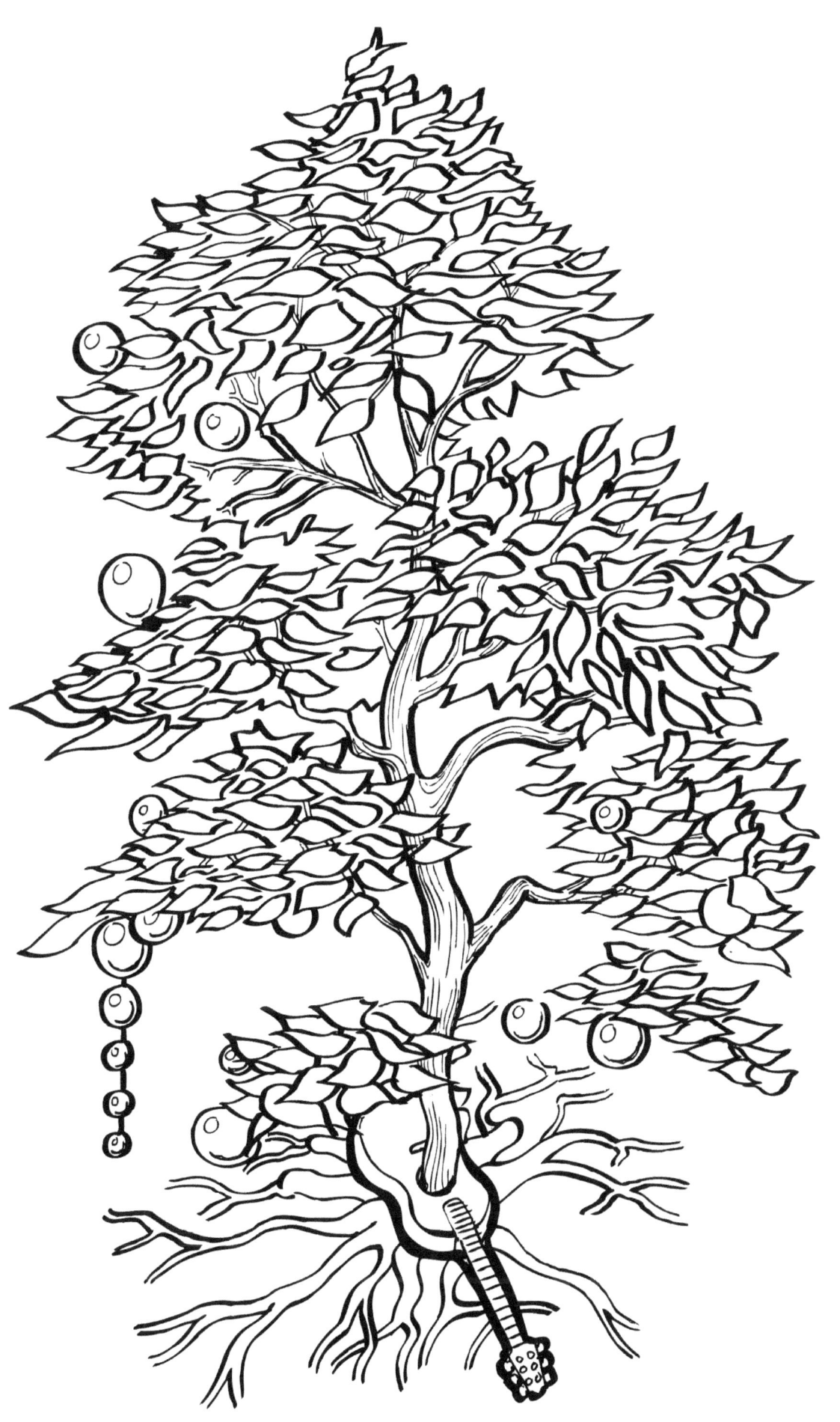

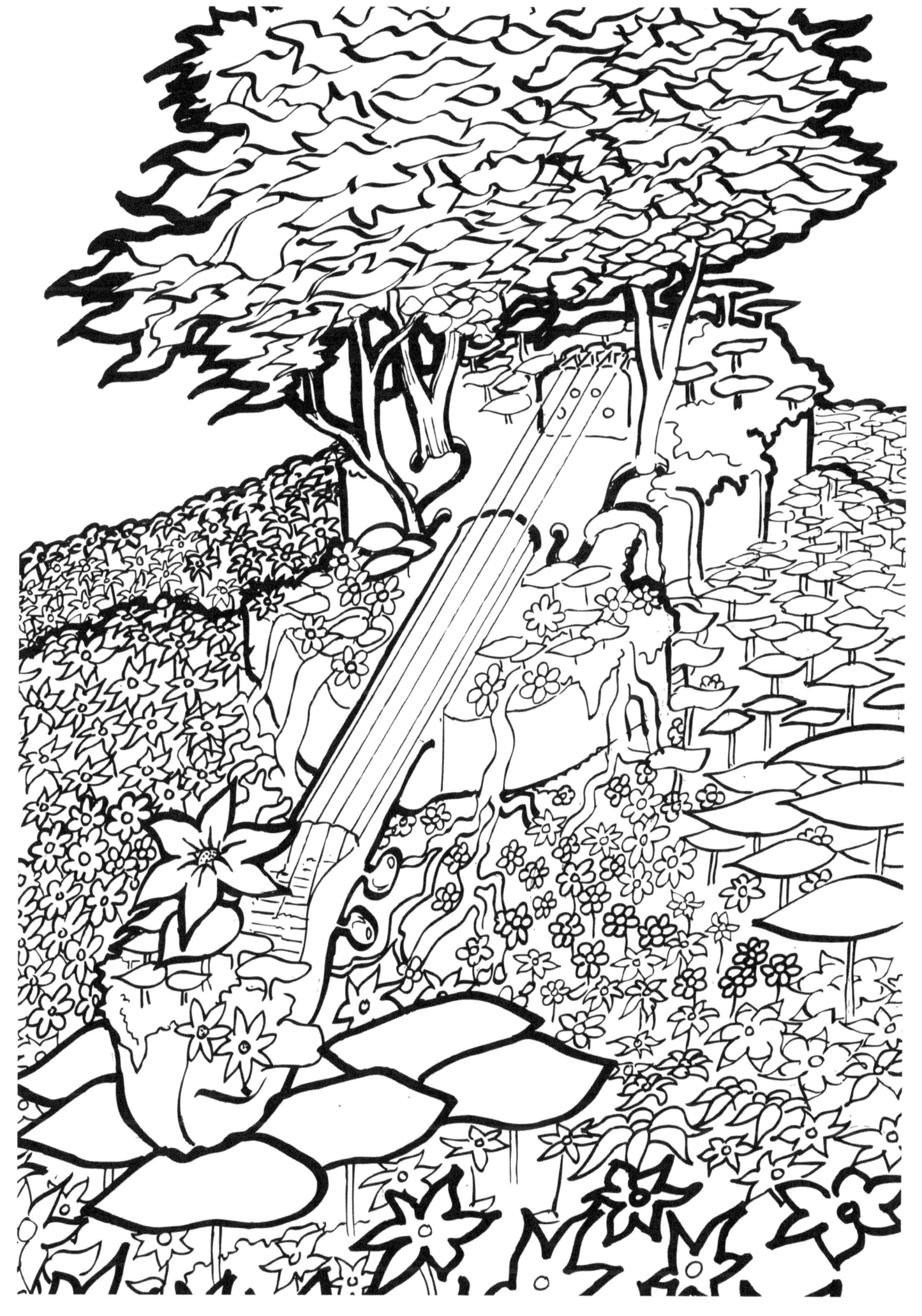

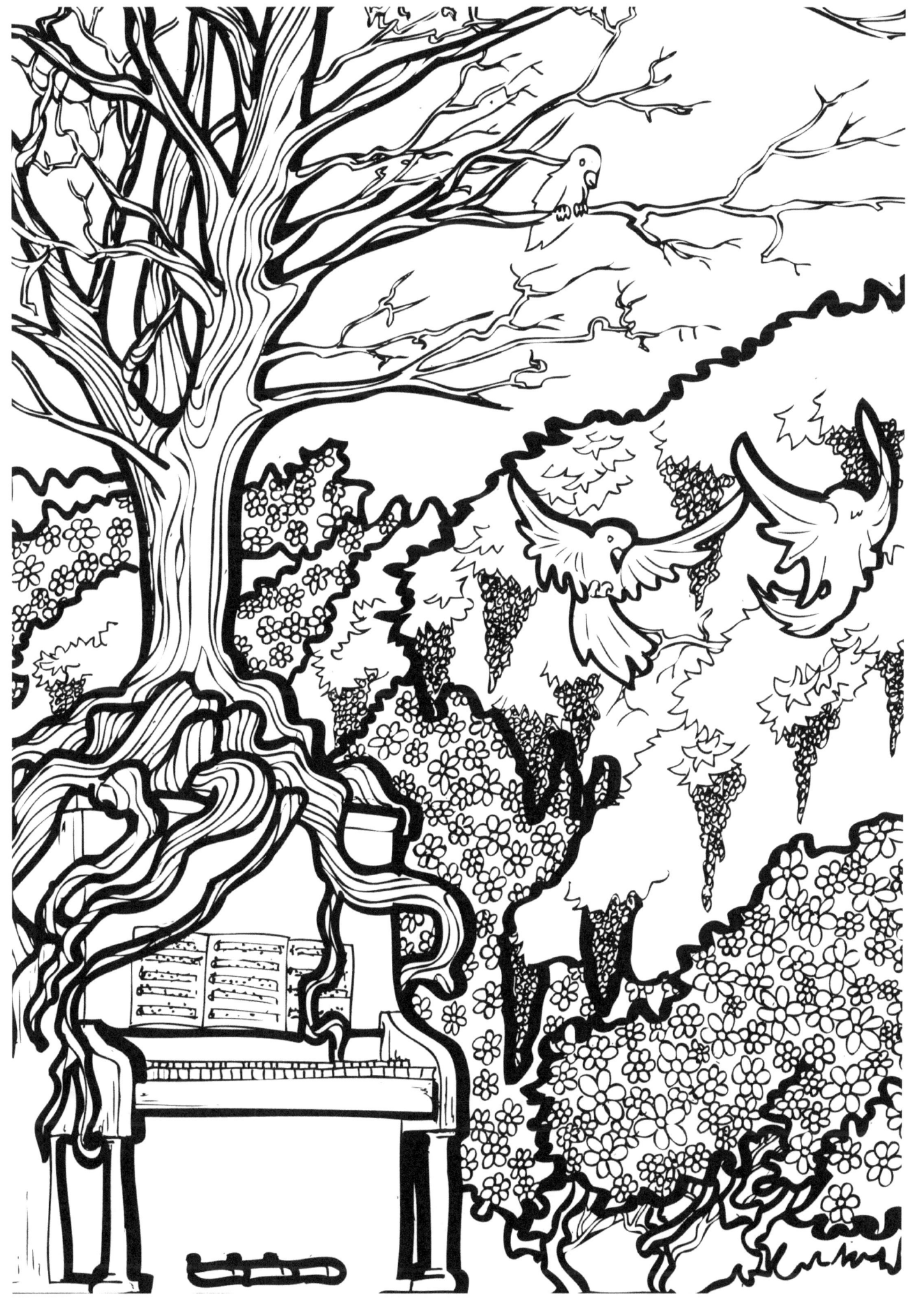

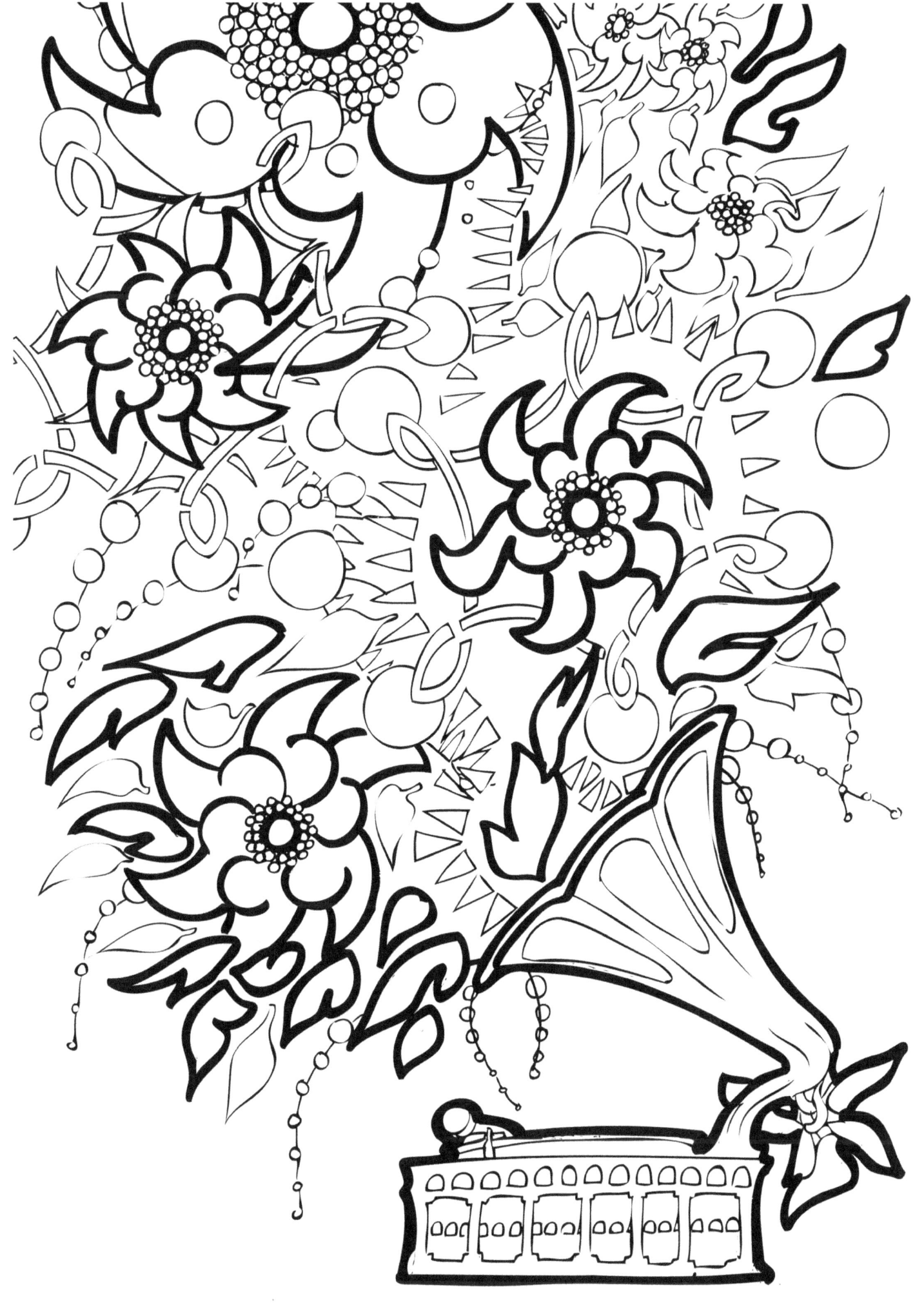

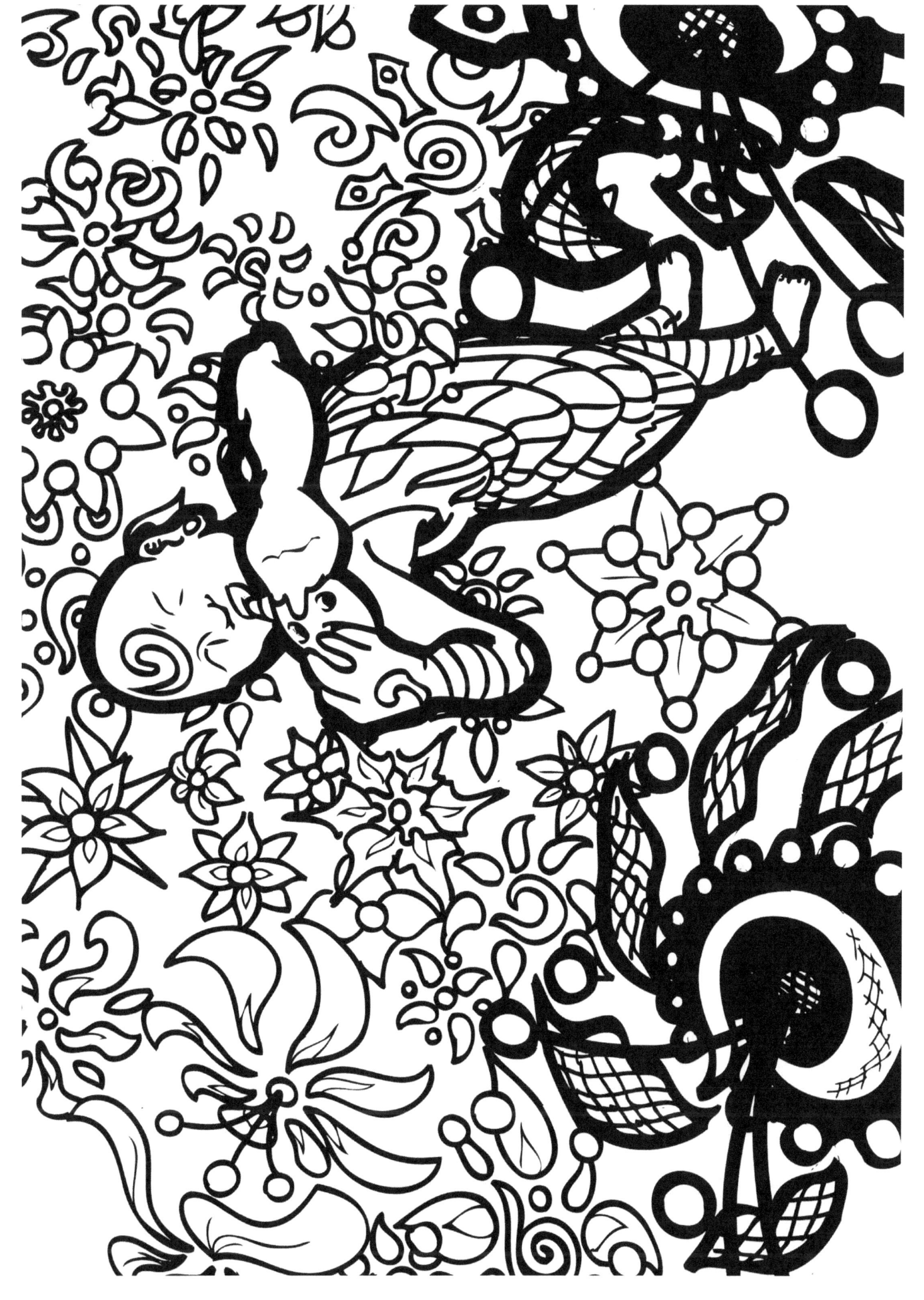

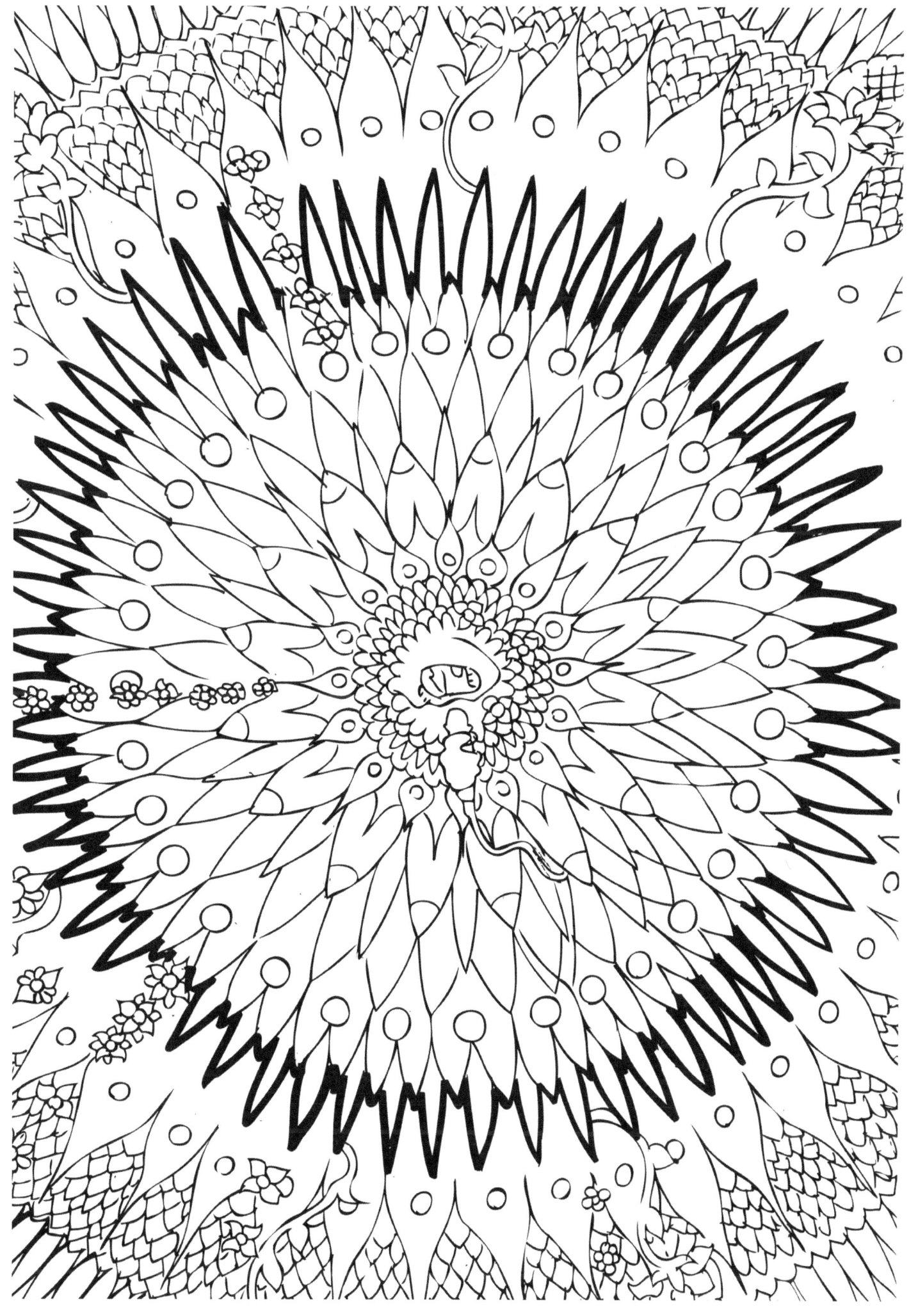

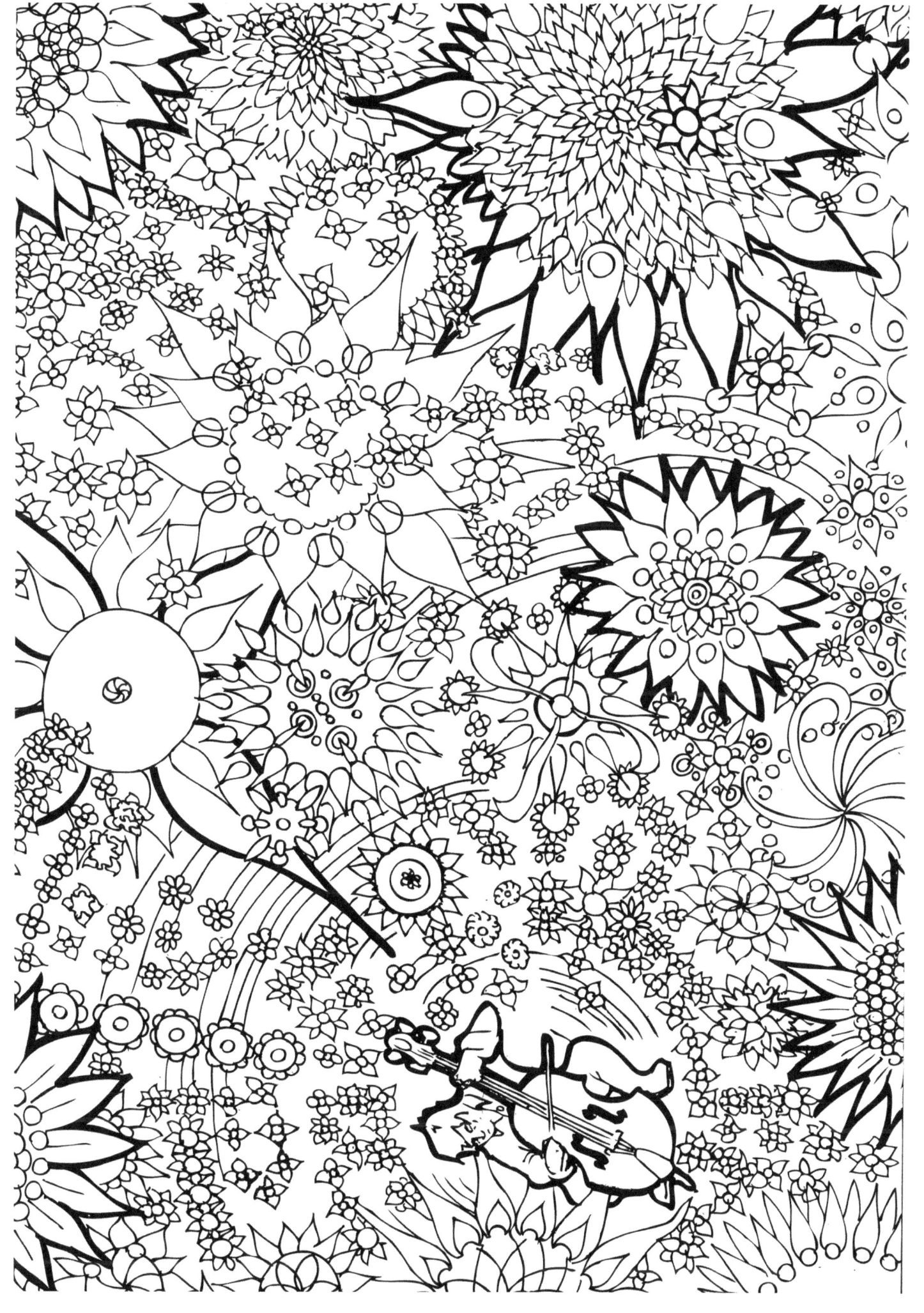

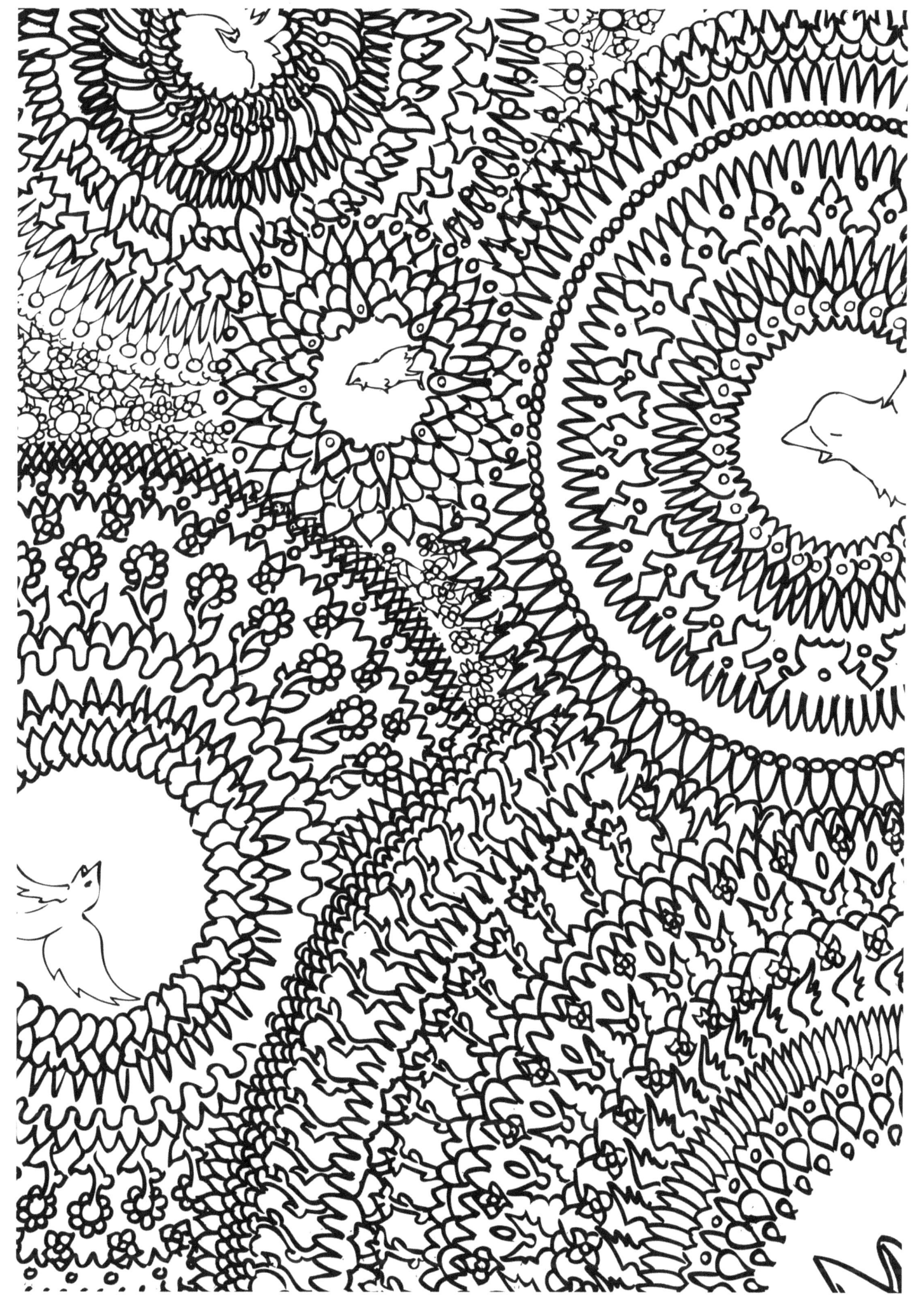

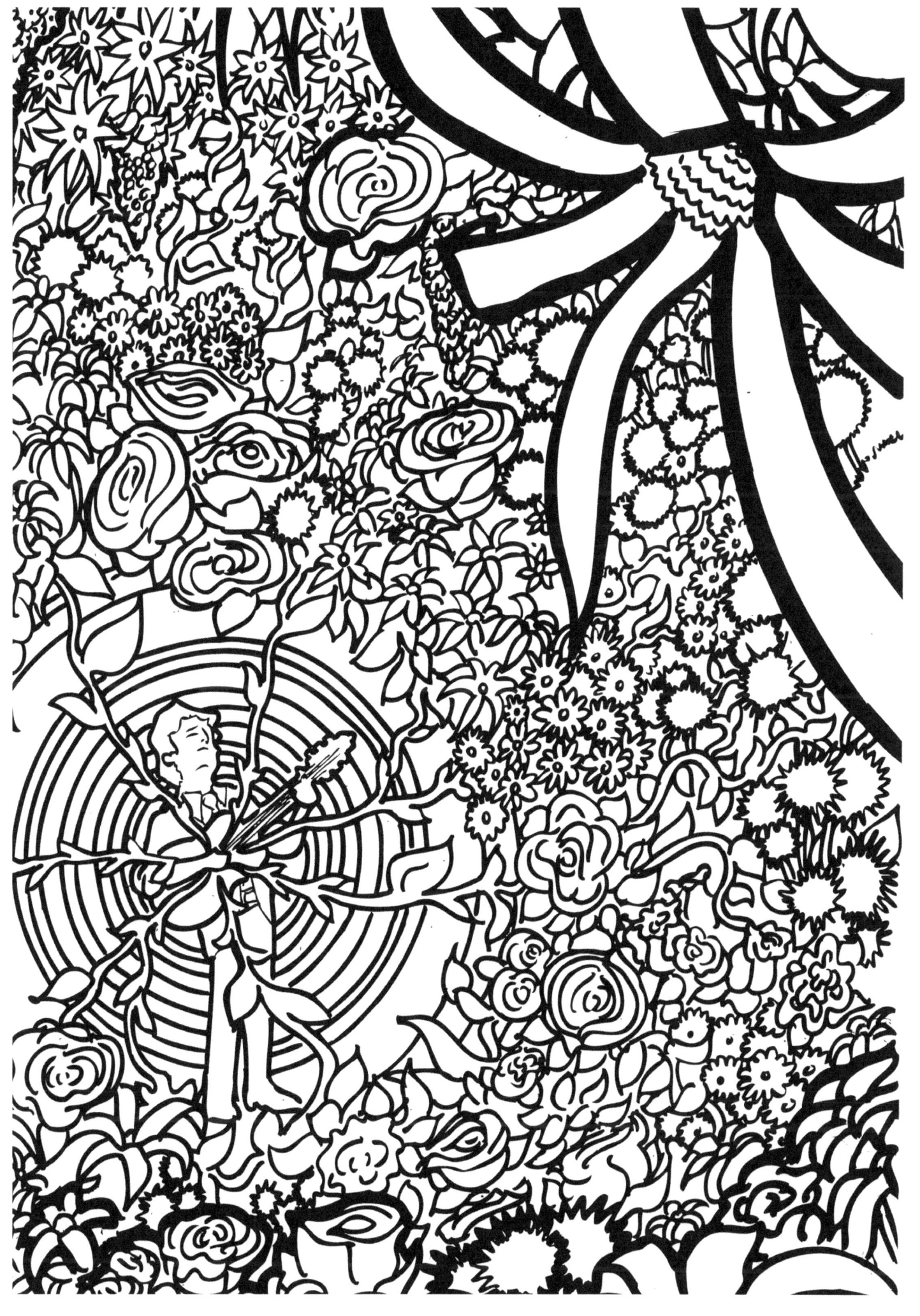

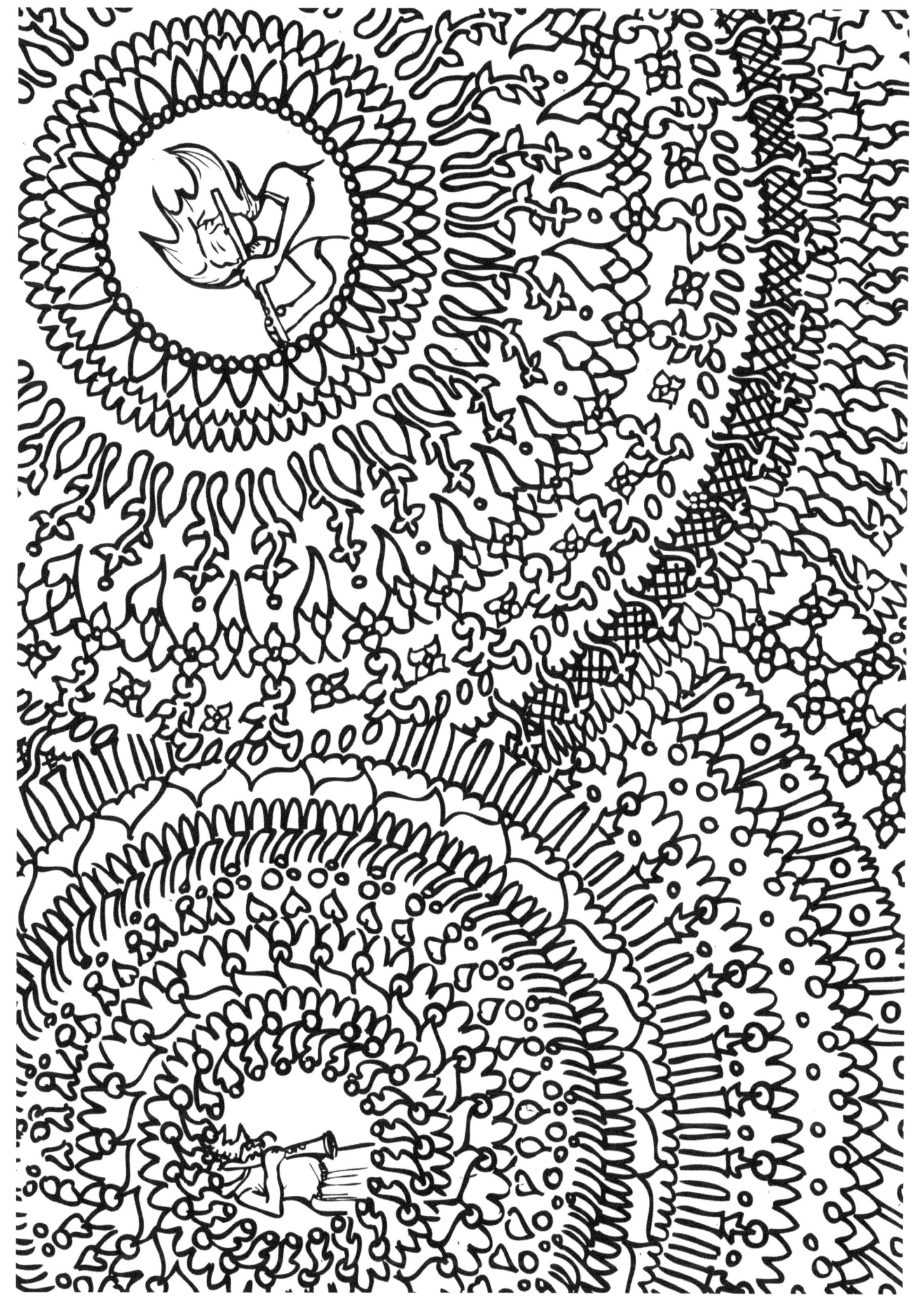

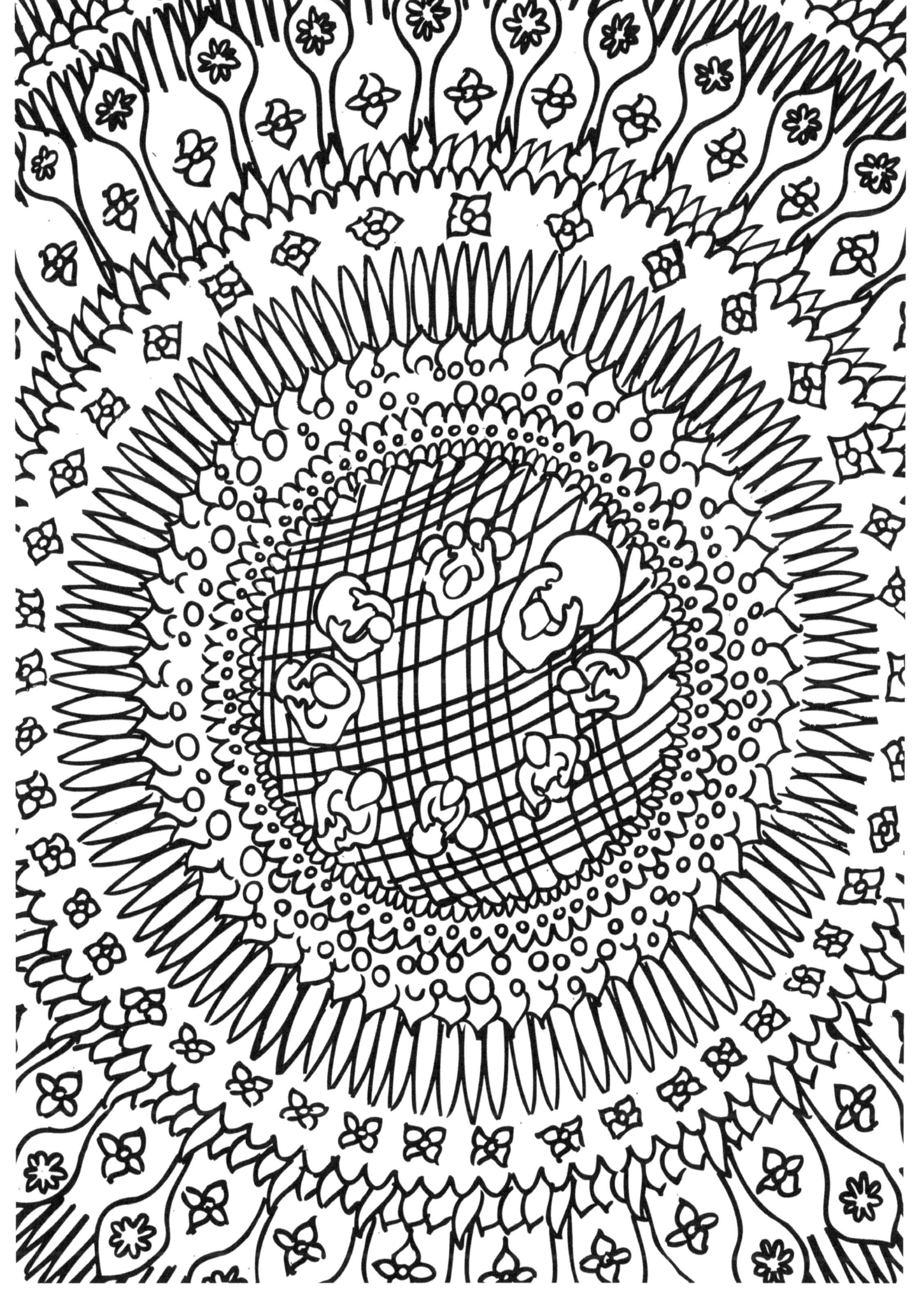

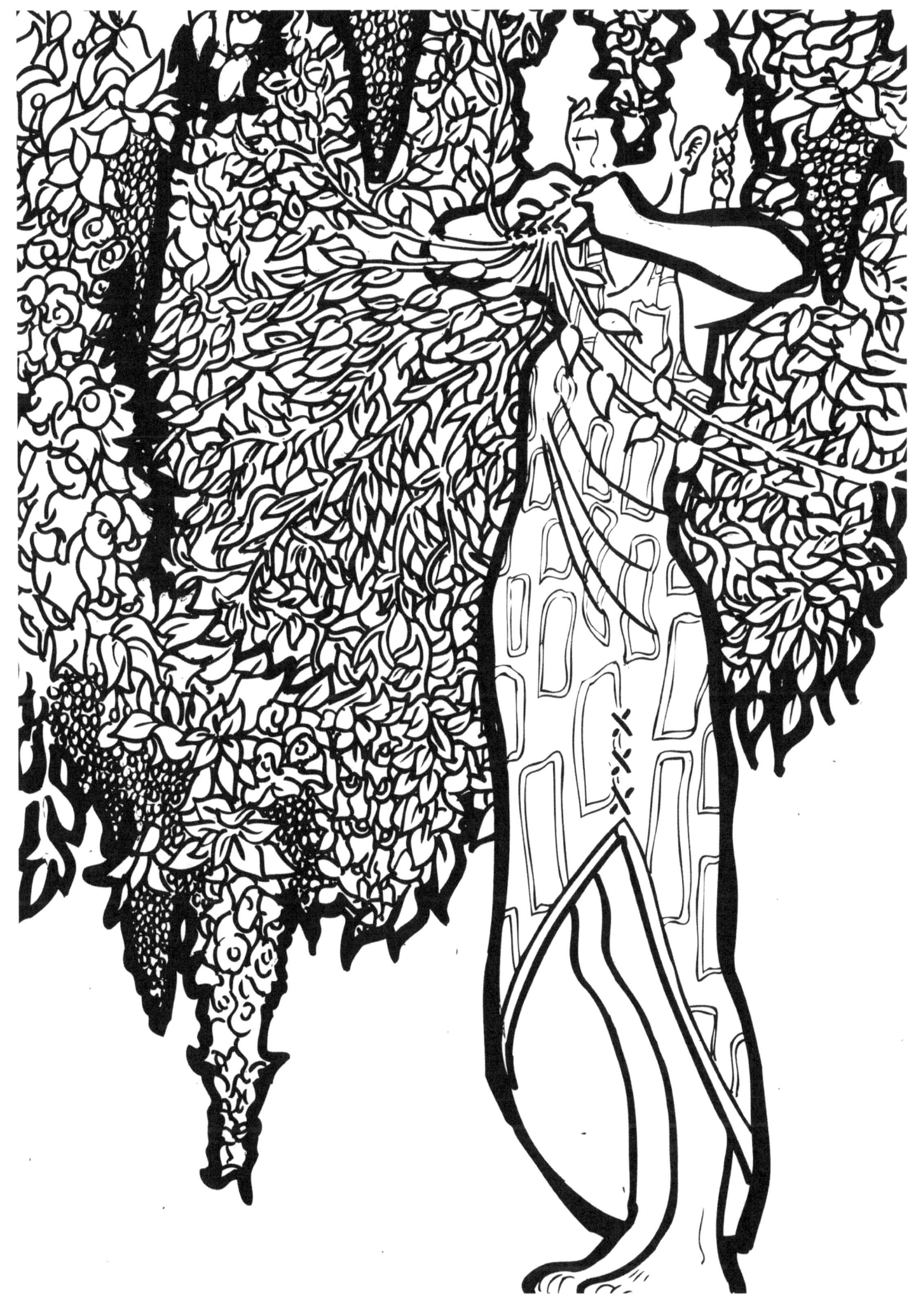

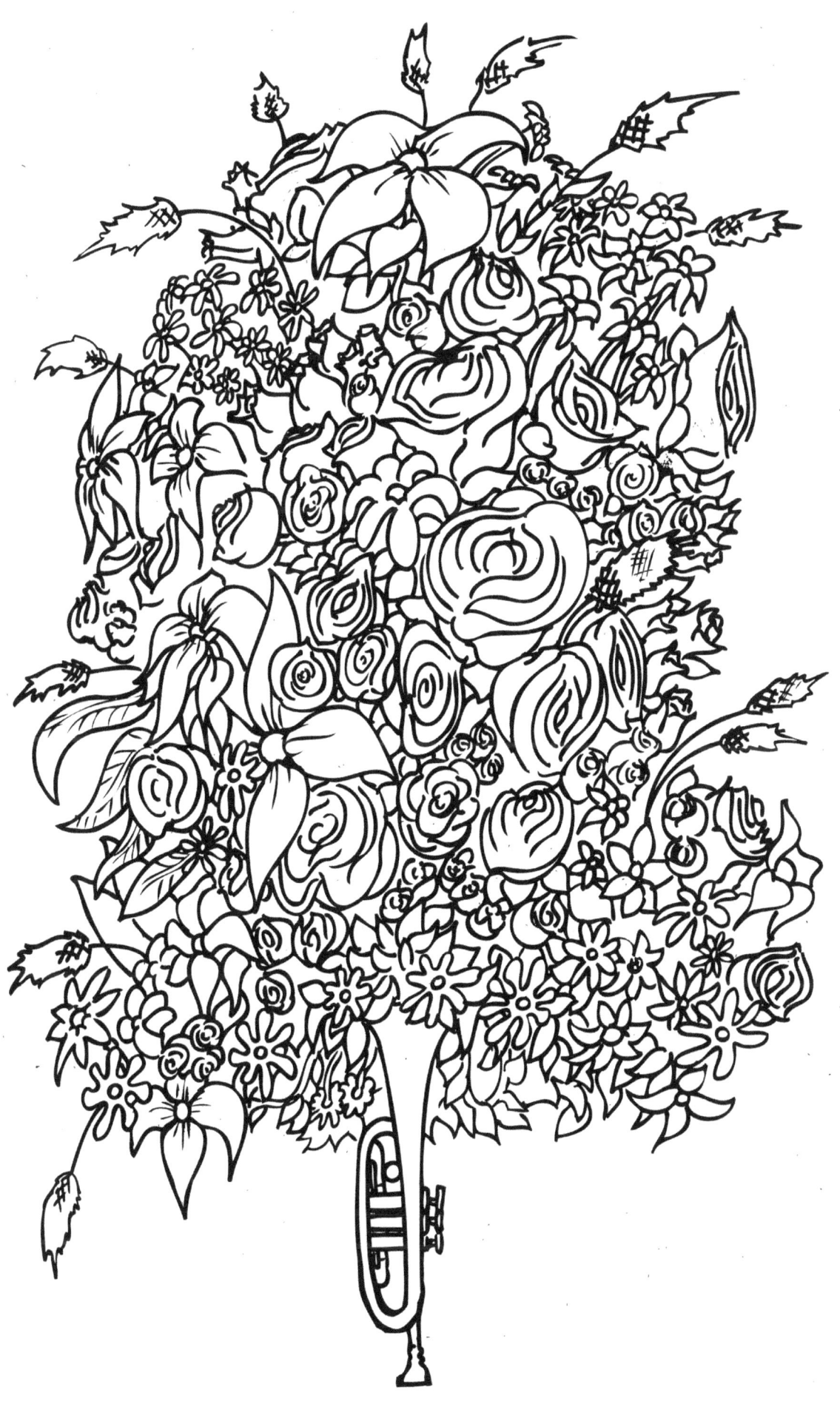

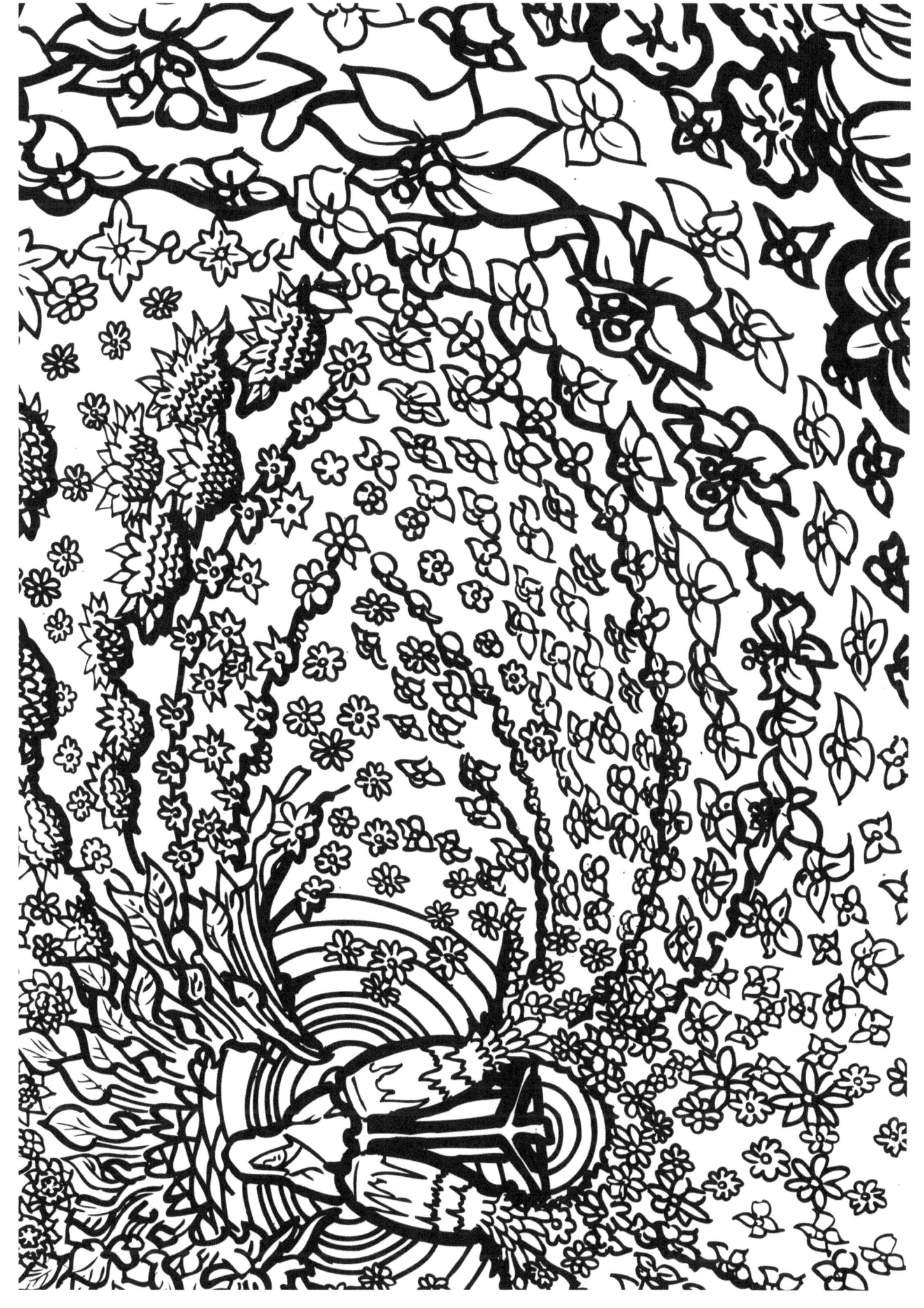

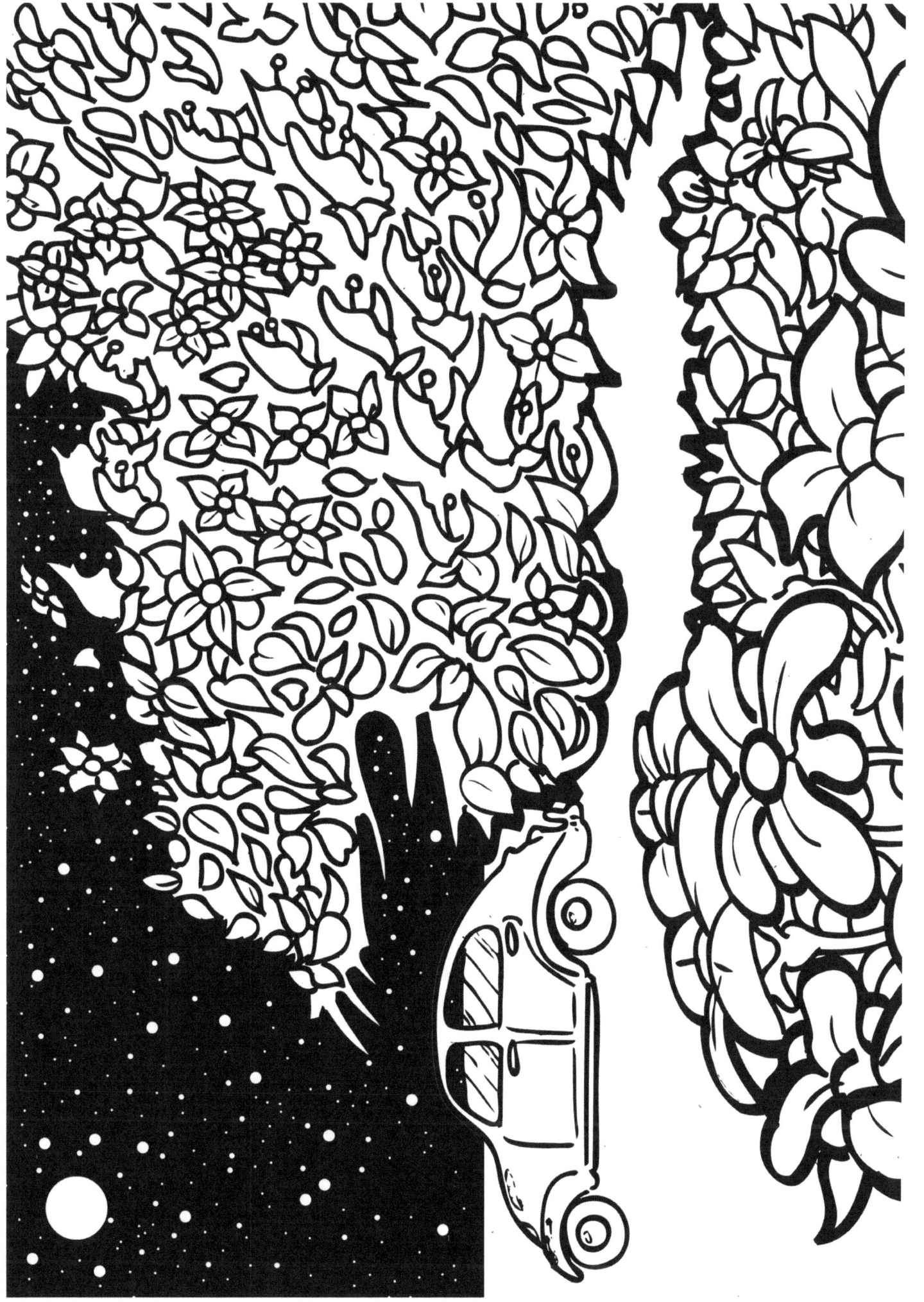

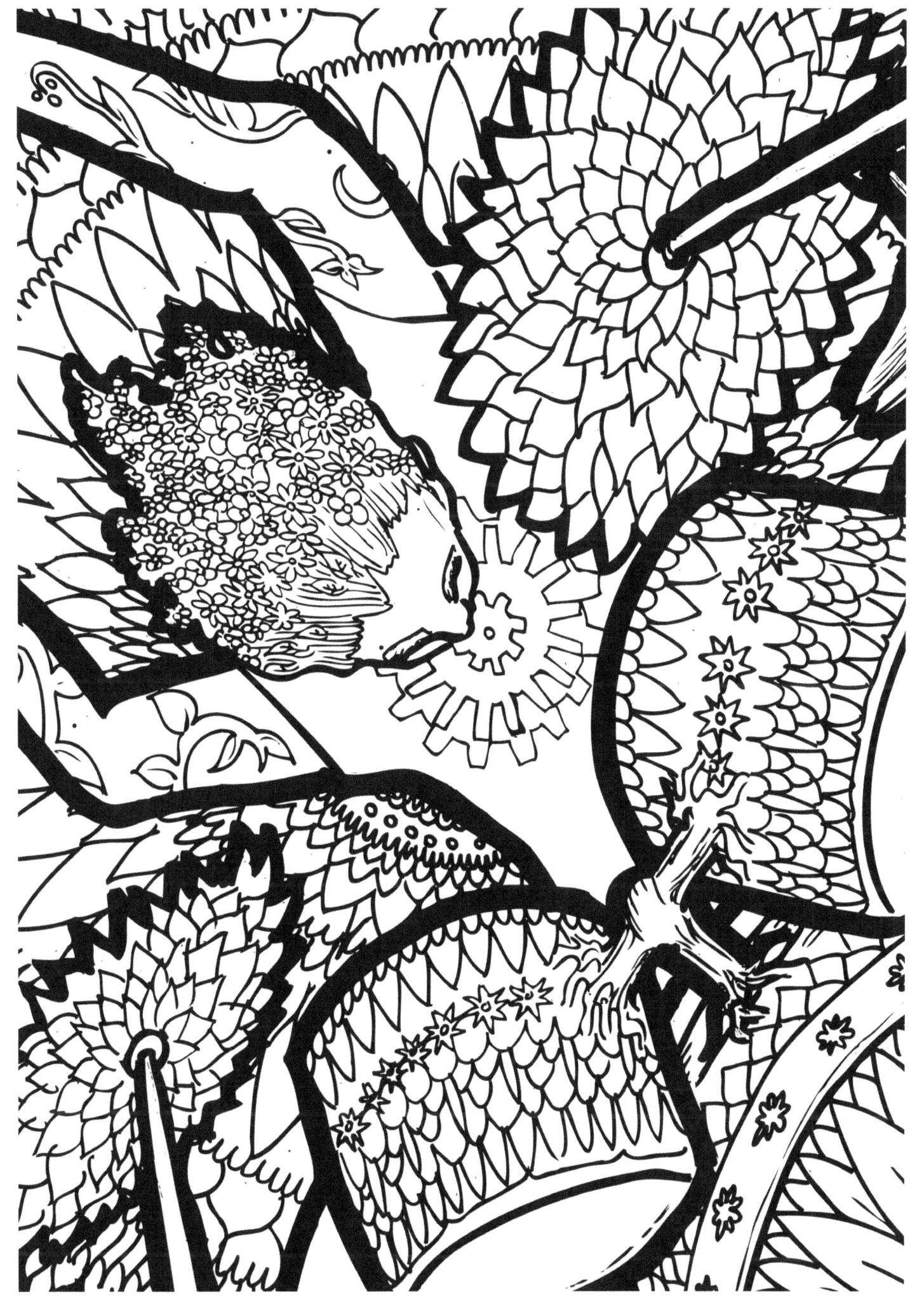

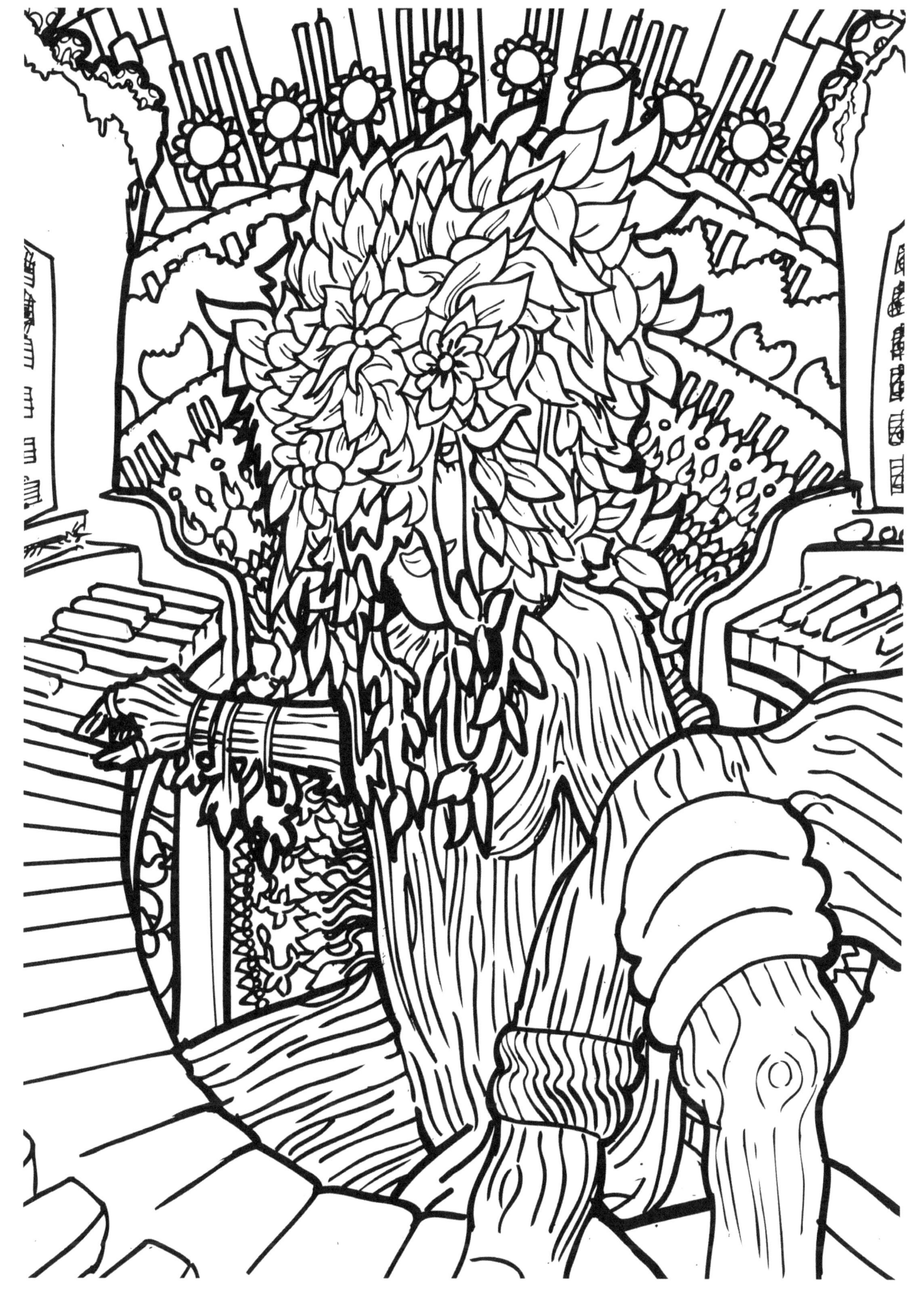

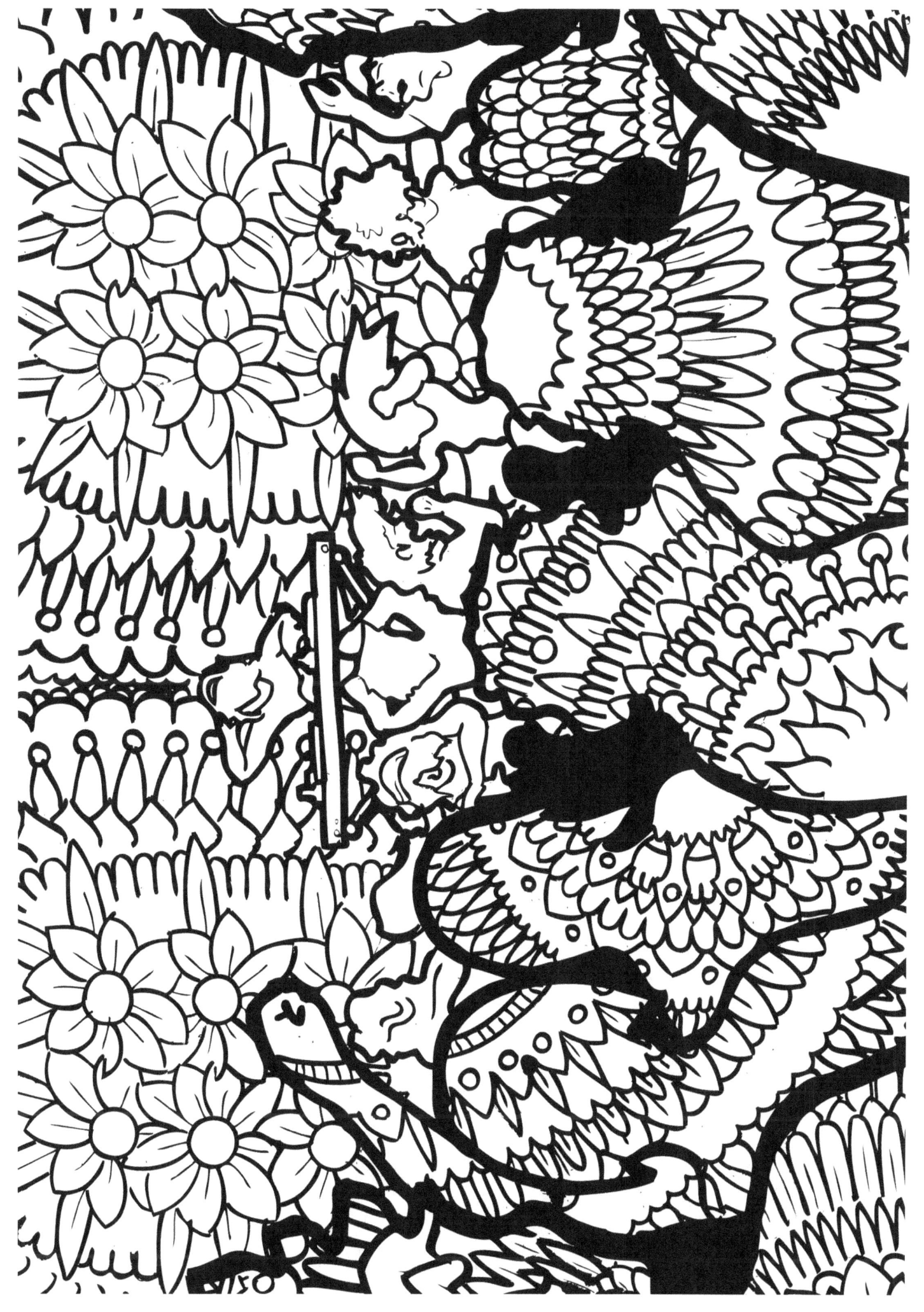

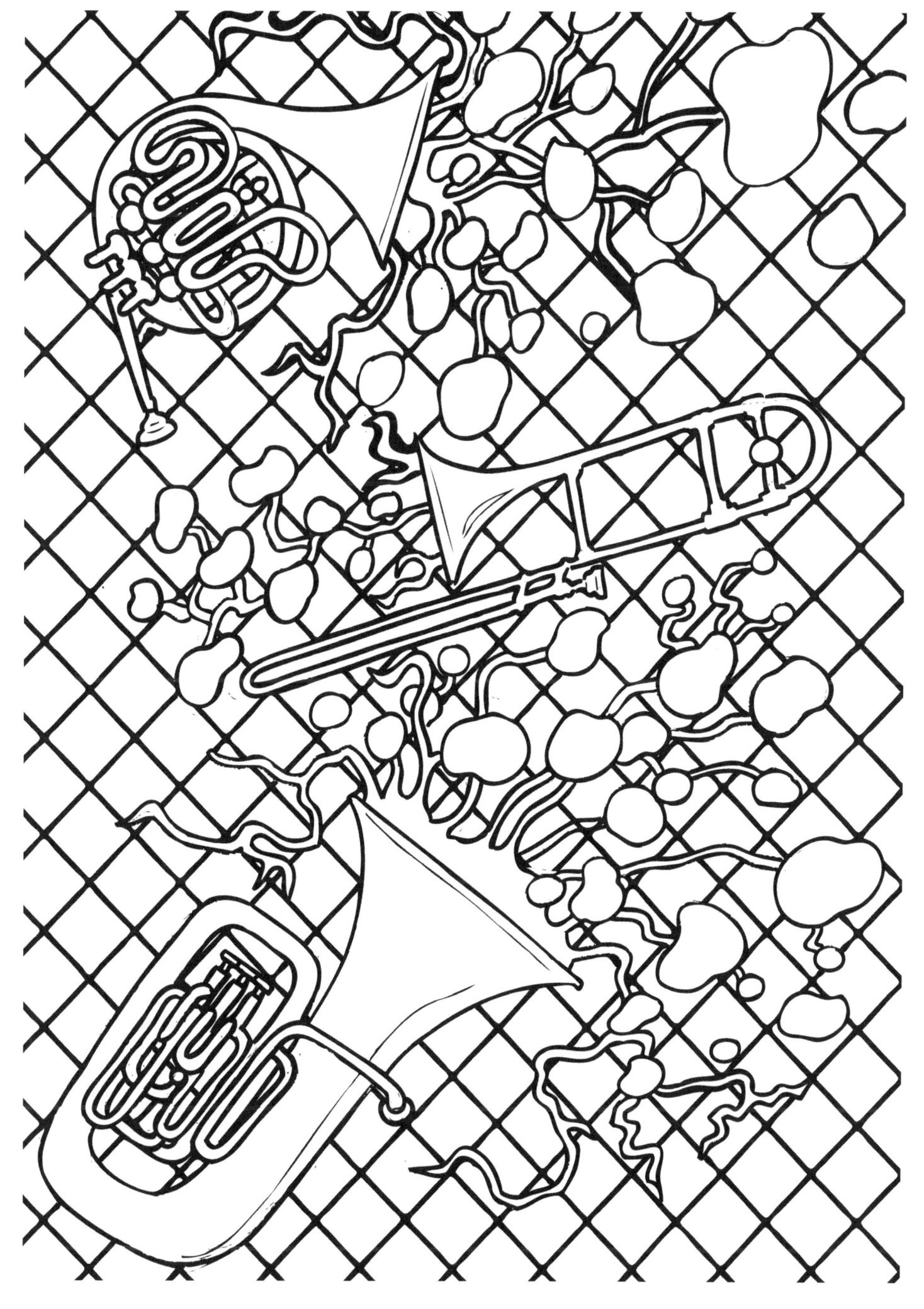

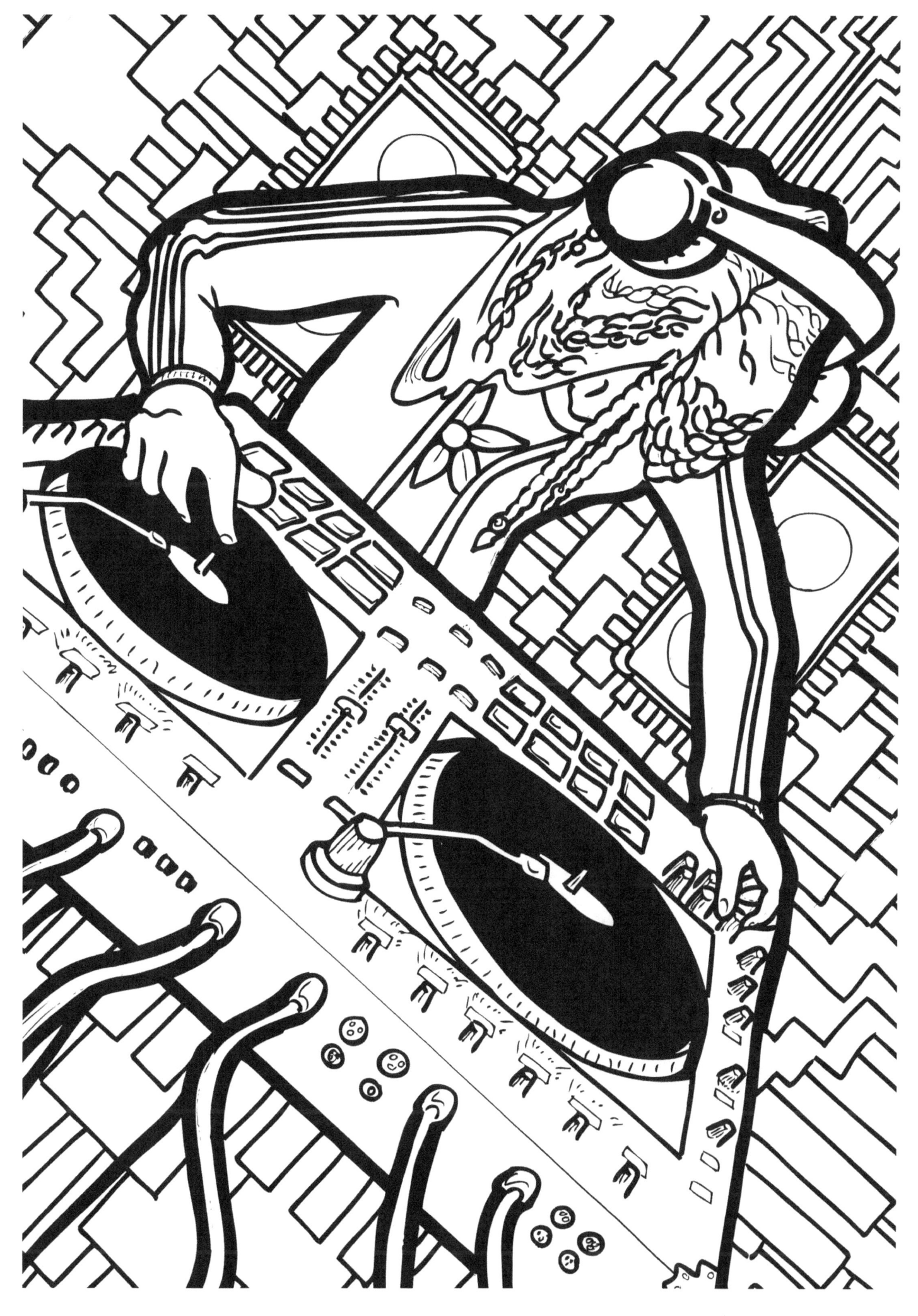

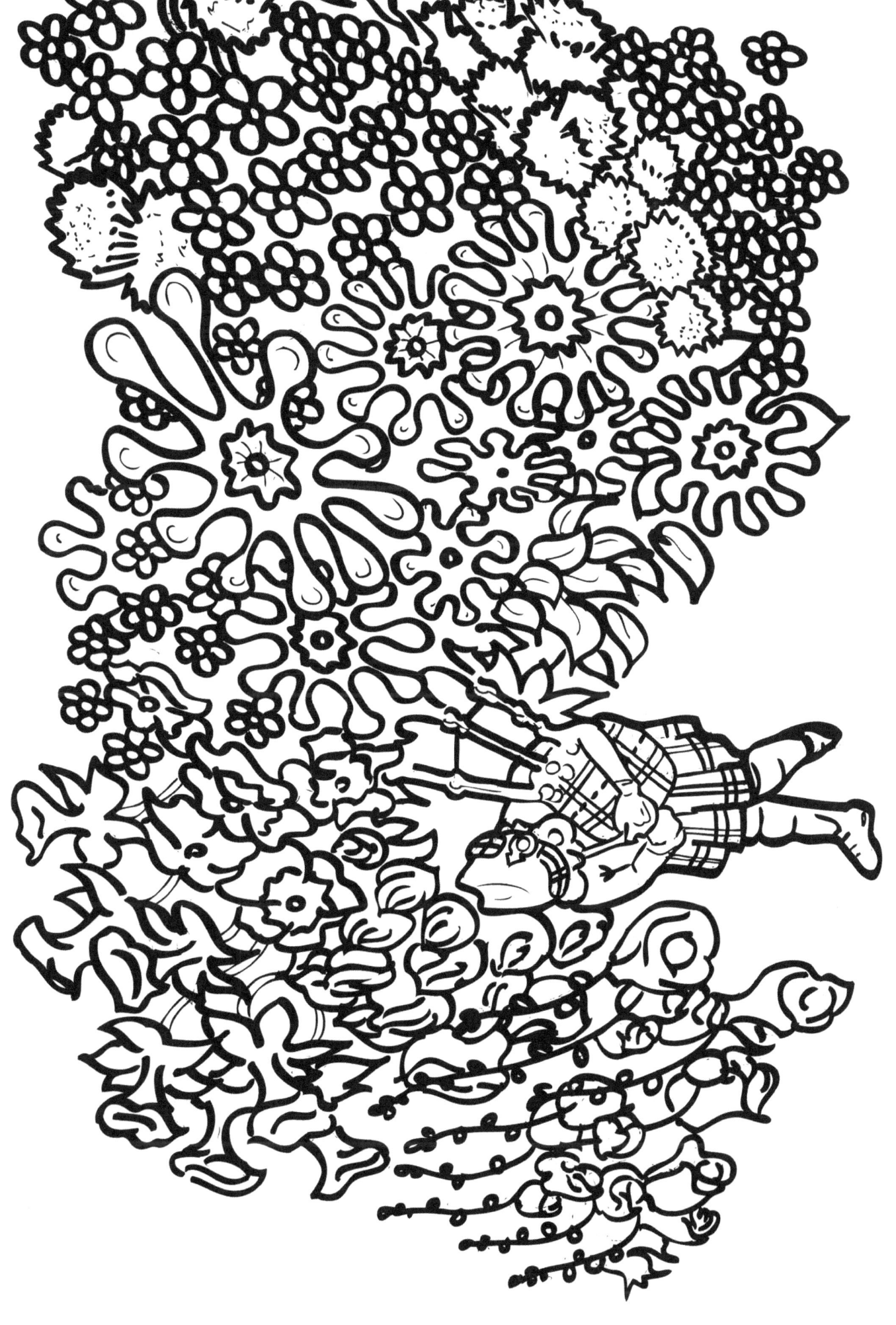